JOURNAL

OF A

STEAM VOYAGE

DOWN THE DANUBE TO

CONSTANTINOPLE,

AND THENCE BY WAY OF

MALTA AND MARSEILLES

TO ENGLAND.

"These Tourists, Heaven preserve us! needs must live
A profitable life." . . . . WORDSWORTH.

LONDON:
PRINTED BY MOYES AND BARCLAY, CASTLE STREET,
LEICESTER SQUARE.
1842.

CONTENTS.

	PAGE
DEPARTURE FOR OSTEND	1
GHENT	1
BRUSSELS	3
LAAKEN	3
MALINES	3
LIEGE	4
AIX-LA-CHAPELLE	5
COLOGNE	6
BONN	7
WIESBADEN	10
FRANKFURT ON THE MAINE	11
NUREMBERG	12
RATISBON	13
LINZ	15
VIENNA	17
PRESBURG	21
PESTH	22
BUDA	23
PETERWARDEIN	27

CONTENTS.

	PAGE
BELGRADE	27
ORSOVA	29
MEHADIA	31
CLADOSNITZA	34
CZERNAVODA	37
KUSTENJÈ	41
CONSTANTINOPLE	43
SMYRNA	72
MALTA	76
VALLETTA	81
SYRACUSE	90
MESSINA	98
NAPLES	102
VESUVIUS	103
POMPEII	107
TEMPLE OF SERAPIS	109
MUSEO BORBONICO	112
CAPUA	115
TERRACINA	116
ROME	119
CIVITA VECCHIA	133
LEGHORN	134
MARSEILLES	135
LYONS	135
PARIS	137
ARRIVAL IN LONDON	138
APPENDIX	139

DOGBERRY.— . . . . "Truly, for mine own part, if I were as tedious as a king, I could find it in my heart to bestow it all on your worship." — *Much Ado about Nothing.*

JOURNAL OF A TOUR.

On *Saturday, June* 26, 1841, at three o'clock in the morning, we left London for Ostend, with our two little boys, and a man and a maid servant. We had rather a rough passage, and arrived at Ostend at half-past five in the afternoon. We dined, and walked in the evening on the Dyke, which affords a fine dry promenade to the lovers of sea-views and sea-breezes. There is but little to detain the tourist at Ostend; but those who have never yet seen any of the carved woodwork for which Belgium is so celebrated will find some good specimens to begin with in the spacious church.

Sunday, June 27.—Sent the children and servants on by the räilway to Brussels, whilst we stopped at Ghent to dine and see the town. The whole place was in a bustle, every one going to the races; English equipages rattling in all directions, and the English tongue predominant. We fell in with several acquaintances, who tried to persuade us to accompany them to the course to witness the sports of the day, but we preferred the quieter scenes of the courts of the Bequinage, and the beauties and riches of the Church of St. Bavon. In this church the pulpit, carved in white marble and oak, is particularly fine. There are many other objects of interest and curiosity in Ghent: few of the cities usually visited by tourists are, on the whole, so well worth seeing.

But in the whirl of steam-power we have actually overlooked the city of Bruges, which we left behind us between Ostend and Ghent. Bruges — where

> "The spirit of antiquity, enshrined
> In sumptuous buildings, vocal in sweet song,
> In picture, speaking with heroic tongue,
> And with devout solemnities entwined,
> Strikes to the seat of grace within the mind."
>
> WORDSWORTH.

Our only excuse is that we visited Bruges not many years ago, when this same journey used to be performed by a conveyance keeping up the notion of "leisure," and "sedate forbearance," and a "decency," more in harmony with the tone of these consecrated cities than the impetuous railway, — I mean the passage boat that was towed along the sleepy canal with an uniform dreamlike motion at the rate of four miles an hour, not to mention the excellent fish dinners served up on board those well-found barks: but these are bygone days, and, agreeably to the new laws of motion, we went on by a late train to Brussels, where we found the children comfortably established at the Hotel (*Belle Vue*).

Monday, June 28.—At Brussels. We visited the Cathedral, which contains objects of the greatest interest and beauty, especially the carved oak pulpit, and an altar-piece designed by Rubens. We also visited the Church of Notre Dame, the Town-Hall, the palace of the States General, the palace of the Prince of Orange, the hotel of the Duke d'Aremberg, and the monument erected to the memory of those who fell in the Revolution of 1830.

In the evening we drove to Laaken, a pretty village near the town. Here Malibran was buried, and an ugly square tomb is erected over her remains. In the church there was an interesting scene of the village children at confession. We then drove as near as we were permitted to the royal residence at Laaken, and returned by the outskirts of the park to Brussels. Left a card for Professor Quetelet at the Observatory.

Tuesday, June 29.—By railway to Malines, and back in the evening. The Cathedral, and the sublime picture of the Crucifixion by Vandyke, are the chief objects of interest here. Nothing can surpass the elegance of the perforated stonework of the Cathedral tower, against which the clock-dial, in light open gilt iron-work, hangs, at a vast height, really like a cobweb. This dial, however, is upwards of fourteen yards in diameter, and the figures denoting the hours are nearly seven feet high, both which measurements we took from the fac-simile of the dial laid down in asphalte in the market-place.

The appearance of desolation that a short time ago

pervaded the town of Malines is beginning to wear off. Here is the central railway station, and new rows of houses are springing up, probably to be soon tenanted by English residents. We also visited a manufactory of the right Mechlin, and admired the light Dutch-gold earrings and ornaments in the shops, which are very tempting; but we could not resist a straw bonnet and cap with lappets, such as are worn here by the peasant girls; a purchase, however, by no means ruinous. We returned the same evening to Brussels. I cannot refrain, before quitting Brussels, from quoting again from Wordsworth: "In Brussels, the modern taste in costume, architecture, &c. has got the mastery; in Ghent there is a struggle; but in Bruges old images are still paramount, and an air of monastic life among the quiet goings on of a thinly peopled city, is inexpressibly soothing."

Wednesday, June 30.—From Brussels to Liege by railway. The chief object of interest at Liege is the Hall of Justice, formerly the Archiepiscopal Palace. The Moorish style of architecture of the interior court is very striking. Here every one will surely prefer Scott's vivid romance of "Quentin Durward" to a more matter-of-fact guide-book. The interior of the Church of St. Jacques has a gorgeous appearance, but the decorations are hardly in good taste. The carved pulpits of Belgium are no more to be seen. The manners and address of the people of Liege are very pleasing. The food and accommodations in general, at our Hotel (*Pavillon Anglais*), were very indifferent, so we walked into the town and dined at a *café*. At ten o'clock at night we left Liege for Aix-la-Chapelle, with two companions, Mr. L—— F——, and Mr. F——, who continued to be our fellow-travellers until the 11th of September.

Thursday, July 1.—At Aix-la-Chapelle, the ancient seat of Charlemagne. We visited the baths, the Redoute, and the churches. The latter are profusely ornamented, but I could not admire them after the Belgian edifices. In the treasury of the Cathedral we saw the "*Petites Reliques*," which, as well as the "*Grandes Reliques*," are deposited there; but the "*Grandes Reliques*" are exhibited to the public only once in seven years, and at other times to none but crowned heads.

We drove in the afternoon to the Louisberg, a hill just out of the town, from whence there is a fine view. A handsome house of public entertainment is built here, which is much frequented; but as the weather was wet and cold the place was quite deserted. The Hotel (*des Quatres Saisons*) at which we were staying was under repair, and was on that account uncomfortable, but it was in other respects well conducted, and the people were very civil.

Friday, July 2.—In a hired carriage from Aix-la-Chapelle to Cologne. We went to the Hotel (*Grosser Rheinberg*), which is most conveniently situated close to the river and to the bridge of boats, the operations connected with which are a constant source of entertainment. It came on to rain when we arrived, with a thick yellow fog, and the river was quite foul and muddy.

Saturday, July 3.—At Cologne. Visited the Cathedral; on entering which stupendous but unfinished edifice every one must feel inclined to break forth with Wordsworth,—

> "O for the help of angels to complete
> This Temple! Angels governed by a plan
> How gloriously pursued by daring man,
> Studious that *He* might not disdain the seat,
> Who dwells in Heaven! But that inspiring heat
> Hath failed; and now, ye Powers! whose gorgeous wings
> And splendid aspect, yon emblazonings
> But faintly picture, 'twere an office meet
> For you, on these unfinished shafts to try
> The midnight virtues of your harmony;—
> This vast design might tempt you to repeat
> Strains that call forth upon empyreal ground
> Immortal fabrics, rising to the sound
> Of penetrating harps and voices sweet!"

We then spent some time in the Church of St. Peter in admiration of Rubens' powerful picture of the crucifixion of that Apostle, and speculated earnestly on the vast collections of bones in the churches of St. Ursula and St. Geryon; after which we sweetened our imaginations, not with an ounce of civet, but with a better thing, some genuine *eau de Cologne.* In the evening the weather became beautifully fine, and we went as far as Bonn by the steamer. We found the Hotel (*Golden Star*) very good.

At night, by the brilliant starlight, a great number of the students, unmindful of Niebuhr and Schlegel, were diverting themselves by marching round the market-place, singing, laughing, and hallooing, bursting out at the same time occasionally into snatches of wild and singularly beautiful choruses with wonderful harmony and effect, tramping all together in strict time to their own music. We mixed with them, and we were of course instantly discovered to be strangers, and at one moment there was a slight indication of the commencement of *a row*, but all ended well and peaceably.

Sunday, July 4.—At Bonn. Interesting procession of the National School children to the Cathedral. They sang in chorus as they passed along, as if harmony was here innate. First came about fifty boys, then as many girls, then a great number of young women, then the priests, and the high-priest with the Host. We all bowed or knelt in the market-place as they passed. The procession must have consisted of many hundreds of persons.

We then walked through the village of Popplesdorf, and up the hill called the Kreutsberg, about two miles from Bonn.

The dead bodies of the monks in the vault of the Conventual Church on the summit of the hill are a great sight here. With an old and very infirm man for our guide, we descended into the vault, and saw them, twenty-five in number, lying in their open wooden coffins in the clothes they wore when alive;

and, strange to say, the sight was not a disgusting one, for the place was perfectly dry, airy, and without smell. The bodies were quite dried up, and their skins resembled leather or parchment. Some had lain there whole centuries. The old man pointed out one of the bodies to us, which he said he had himself seen deposited there more than sixty years before. He was very asthmatic, and was unable to surmount the last few steps leading out of the vault without the help of a stout young girl who had placed herself so as to be in readiness to assist him. Whilst he stood, both figuratively and literally, with one foot in the grave, clinging to her for support, the group presented a vivid picture of youthful vigour standing between old age and the King of Terrors.

Here, too, we were shewn a flight of stairs said to have been those which led up to the Judgment-Hall of Pilate, still stained with the blood that fell from our Saviour's brow; a tradition which is also reported of the "*Scala Santa*" at Rome.

We went on in the afternoon to the ruined castle of Godesberg, which is well worth a visit, as is also the quiet little watering-place close at hand. Nothing can exceed the beauty of the view from thence, looking over the country and across the Rhine to the Seven Mountains. After rambling about, and tasting the water of the mineral spring, we went on to Königswinter (*Hôtel de Berlin*), where we remained for the night. But the evening was most lovely, and we could not resist the temptation of an excursion to the summit of the Drachenfels before we retired to rest; during the ascent and descent the views are beautiful. The river, however, as you look directly down upon it from the summit, takes somewhat the appearance of a canal: the best view is obtained by looking up the river towards the Island of Nonnenworth.

Monday, July 5.—Bathed in the river early in the morning, and at half-past seven we started for St. Goar by the steamer. The beauties of the Rhine, the perpetual " dance of objects," occupied us all the way. We stopped at St. Goar, at the Hotel (*Fleur de Lys*), and then walked up to the Castle of Rhein-fels. It is a ruin of great extent, and is very well worth seeing, and forms a principal feature in the lovely scenery. We were perpetually catching fresh and delightful points of view as we walked and scrambled about.

Hallam, speaking of the state of society in the middle ages, says:—

" The more ravenous feudal lords descended from their fortresses to pillage the wealthy traveller, or shared in the spoil of inferior plunderers. * * * Germany appears to have been, upon the whole, the country where downright robbery was most unscrupulously practised by the great. Their castles, erected on almost inaccessible heights among the woods, became the secure receptacles of predatory bands, who spread terror over the country. From these barbarian lords of the dark ages, as from a living model, the romancers are said to have drawn their giants and other disloyal enemies of true chivalry."

And again in the same work, speaking of Germany:

"A very large proportion of the rural nobility lived by robbery. Their castles, as the ruins still bear witness, were erected upon inaccessible hills, and in defiles that command the public road. An Archbishop of Cologne having built a fortress of this kind, the governor inquired how he was to maintain himself, no revenue having been assigned for that purpose. The prelate only desired him to remark that the castle was situated near the junction of four roads."

In the evening we walked along the banks of the noble river, admiring the volume and torrent of the water, and the whirlpools dreaded by raft-owners. At night we were amused by the echoes of a French horn, played for our edification by a village professor.

Tuesday, July 6. — Walked to the village of Petersberg up the gorge called by courtesy the Swiss valley, on the side of the river opposite to St. Goar. Then by the steamer to Biebrick, and from thence in a carriage to Wiesbaden. Heavy rain came on, and I was attacked with a feverish cold.

Wednesday, July 7. — At Wiesbaden (*English Hotel*). Remained at home all day.

Thursday, July 8. — We are not much pleased with Wiesbaden: it is hot, close, and expensive. Wandering round the shops of the Kursaal, and through the assembly and gaming rooms, is an operation which soon becomes wearisome. Yet Wiesbaden is a place of extensive and ancient repute, and the environs are lovely, and the natural hot springs are exceedingly curious.

Friday, July 9.—To Frankfurt on the Maine in the afternoon by railway (*Hôtel de Russie*). Here we found the best *table d' hôte* we have yet met with, and excellent Rudesheimer, of which divine potation

> "Fecundi calices quem non fecere disertum?"—HORACE.

Frankfurt is a very fine town, and it struck me as somewhat resembling Ghent.

Saturday, July 10.—We called on Mr. Koch the banker, who received us, as he receives every one, with the greatest kindness and civility, and invited us to his house in the evening. We amused ourselves all day with the public walks and sights of Frankfurt, of which, perhaps, the chief are Dannecker's celebrated statue of Ariadne, and the burying-ground. The Ariadne is the property of Monsieur Bethman; she is represented as reclining on a leopard:

> "Illa (nec invideo) fruitur meliore marito,
> Inque capistratis tigribus alta sedet."
> OVID, *Epist. II.* 80.

The bronze copies of the Ariadne sold in Frankfurt are heavy to the eye as well as to the pocket.

The burying-ground is about a mile out of the city; I walked thither with a young German with whom I fell in company accidentally, and who spoke English perfectly well. Connected with the burying-ground are a series of chambers arranged for the reception of persons apparently dead, with all kinds of apparatus for resuscitation, which I was informed had hardly ever been used, and was therefore surprised to find in complete order.

We then walked over the burial-ground, and reached a point which commanded a view of the whole, together with the range of country beyond, towards the Taunus hills, then glowing in the sunset; close by on our right, adjoining the cemetery, was a corn-field, and the thought came across me that there was a crop sown on *both* sides of the wall. Having been conducted round the whole, we wished our guide good evening, and walked back together to Frankfurt.

Sunday, July 11.—Weather very cold with heavy rain. Preparations for departure.

Monday, July 12.—We left the children at Frankfurt with the man-servant, in order to return to England by the next boat down the Rhine to Rotterdam; and started in the morning from Frankfurt for Würtzburg in the Eil-wagen. The forest of Spessart, part of the ancient Hercynian forest, and the ferry at Lang-fürth, were among the most interesting features of our journey. We arrived at Würtzburg at night, in about twelve hours from Frankfurt; and started again the same night for Nuremberg.

Tuesday, July 13.—We arrived at Nuremberg at about noon, but remained in this celebrated ancient city only for a few hours. The streets are fine and wide, without the gloom that usually hangs over old

German towns, so that the fantastic and in many instances beautiful architecture of the houses is seen to great advantage. We left Nuremberg for Ratisbon, and arrived there about midnight. We were overtaken by heavy rain with thunder and lightning, at about seven in the evening.

Wednesday, July 14.—At Ratisbon; a remarkable and ancient city. Funeral service and procession for the Bishop of Ratisbon, who was buried in the Cathedral this day. The procession through the streets was tedious, but the whole effect very striking, with an immense assemblage of the clergy.

The town-hall, torture-chamber, and dungeons, are very curious. The instruments of torture are nearly perfect; the stone weights that were attached to the feet of wretches suspended from the ceiling and thus racked perpendicularly were such as I could with difficulty lift with one hand. The horizontal rack wanted but new ropes to put it in working order. In the Council, or Diet Chamber, we were shewn a book entitled, " Constitutio Criminalis Theresiana," *Vienna*, 1769; in which were plates of the instruments of torture, and of their application, with some elaborate methods of tying the arms and fingers tight with small cord, not unlike, at first sight, representations of the application of surgical bandages, but in reality how different!

The dungeons are quite unlike the airy, moonshiny cells of romance; they are dark, close, wainscoted rooms, in the solid stone building, some eight feet square, conveying no idea but that of blind and hopeless captivity. Underneath those into which we entered are others, into which the prisoners were lowered and secured by iron gratings, through which we threw down pieces of lighted paper to afford us a view of these horrible pits for the living.

The gate of the Scotch Benedictine Church appeared to us as very remarkable for the grotesque Orientalism of its architecture. Some of the devices are figured in Dibdin's " German Tour."

The weather was beautiful, and we walked round a pleasant public garden, where several public monuments are erected, and among them one to the memory of Kepler, who died here. We met with no English, and the people were very civil, and took much notice of G———. The antique gloom of Ratisbon is very striking. The bridge over the Danube is a curious structure, and the view from it very fine. Hotel (*Golden Angel*).

Thursday, July 15.—At five o'clock in the morning, in a pour down of rain, we left Ratisbon in the steamer for Linz. We soon came to some rocky hills on our left, about a mile from the river, on one of which the Valhalla (the modern German Parthenon) occupies a most commanding situation. It continued to rain heavily, and the hills were partially shrouded in mist. The heights were all wooded. We then came to Donaustauff, where the scenery became more interesting. Between nine and ten o'clock the weather cleared up as we approached a fine range of lofty cultivated hills on the left bank, with villages and churches interspersed. We then came to Degendorf. This place is backed by lovely and imposing scenery, not unlike what I remember to have seen in the county of Wicklow. There was a fine effect of mist and heavy rain far up the valley inland. At half past twelve we reached Passau. It is, apparently, a large town, and is singularly beautiful as seen from the river. The Danube here receives the river Inn as a tributary. The citadel stands finely on a hill clothed with wood. Passau certainly exceeds Coblentz in beauty. On leaving Passau we passed for several miles through a noble defile, with a mixture of rock, wood, and verdure, down to the water's edge, reminding me of some scenes near Keswick. The scenery is altogether wilder and more satisfactory than that of the Rhine; the perpetual verdure is a new and delightful feature; the only drawback here, as on the Rhine, is the want of transparency in the water. We arrived at Linz in twelve hours. The distance between Linz and Ratisbon by the road is 127 miles; I conclude, therefore, that by the river the distance must be nearly 200 miles. In the evening we walked about the lovely environs of Linz; the hills in the neighbourhood are of considerable height. Hotel (*Golden Lion*).

Friday, July 16.—Left Linz for Vienna by a fine steamer at six in the morning. We descended the river at an astonishingly rapid rate, and arrived at the landing place at three o'clock, in nine hours from Linz.

Even where the banks are low, and the country in the immediate neighbourhood is flat, the nature of the river itself, which is full of islands, shallows, and sunken rocks, is still such as to keep alive the attention of both passengers and pilots; we had three men at the wheel for several miles. Sometimes the river assumes the appearance of a lake full of islands. The defiles are wooded down to the water's edge, with a mixture of rock and fine grassy slopes, and perhaps a strip of cultivated land. Here are also rocky heights crowned with churches, convents, and castles, now in ruins, once the feudal dwellings of robber knights or wreckers of the Danube. As subjects for the pencil we particularly remarked the town of Enns and the Castle of Nieder Wallsee.

We then came to the celebrated rapid and whirlpool, the Strudel and Wirbel. Here the scenery, in unbounded variety, exquisite harmony, and considerable grandeur, perhaps exceeded any thing I ever saw before. As we shot down the torrent, we saw three or four rude barges, with capital teams of good-looking horses, struggling against the stream along the rugged towing path, the drivers urging them, and saluting us, with wild cries and gestures.

Next we came to the convent of Mölk. The pencil alone can convey any idea of the beauty of this vast and noble structure enthroned on its rocky eminence, with the Danube winding round its base: I certainly never saw any thing so superb. Next came the Castles of Aggstein and Durrenstein; the latter said to have undoubtedly been the prison of Richard Cœur-de-Lion; next rose to view, at a short distance from the river, the majestic Convent of Gottweich, scarcely inferior to the Convent of Mölk. The wonderful beauties of the Danube have hitherto surprised and delighted us; nothing can exceed the effect of the deep cool verdure of the precipitous defiles; and where the view is more open, the eye is not confined to the immediate neighbourhood of the river, but enjoys exquisite views, comprising several distinct distances, often extending a great way inland.

The extreme beauty of the scenery falls off as you approach Vienna; yet there are some bold hills on the right bank, the spurs of the Noric Alps. We disembarked at Nussdorf, and went on to Vienna. Hotel (*London-Stadt*).

Saturday, July 17.—At Vienna—the Cathedral—Prince Lichstenstein's collection of pictures—the Prater—heat of the weather intense.

Sunday, July 18.—Divine service at the Church of St. Peter—walked about the town—in the evening to the public gardens with Strauss's band. The heat to-day was very extraordinary; the sky was cloudless, with a violent hot wind from the south-west: shade afforded no refreshment: underneath a gateway, or in any other situation where there was a strong current of air, the heat was greatest of all.*

Monday, July 19.—Royal tombs at the Church of the Capucins—palace of the Archduke Charles—cabinet of minerals—drive to the field of Wagram—to the swimming school.

Tuesday, July 20.—Occupied in the morning with small purchases; then to the Belvidere Palace, where, amongst an infinity of curiosities of various descriptions, we saw the salt-cellar made for Francis I. by Benvenuto Cellini, and described by him in his own memoirs.

In the evening to the public gardens, where there was a ball, with Lanner's band. It was a beautiful and entertaining sight. The dancing consisted entirely of waltzes and gallopades. We thought the gentlemen performed much better than the ladies. The gardens were lighted up very prettily, and parties were sitting under the trees, whose branches were hung with lamps, whilst bonnets and shawls suspended on the boughs mixed their gay colours with the illuminated foliage. There were probably a thousand people in the ball-room and gardens, and at least an equal number were regaling at a cheaper rate outside the doors of admittance. Universal order and good-humour seemed to prevail.

* In Galignani's newspaper of August 3d this great heat is mentioned as having been felt throughout Europe, and Fahrenheit's thermometer is there stated to have stood at Vienna at 102° in the shade.

Wednesday, July 21.—In the morning to the arsenal, which is full of curiosities, and to one or two galleries of pictures. To the Opera in the evening.

Thursday, July 22.—Museum of natural history—more pictures—palace and gardens of Schön-brunnen—public gardens with Lanner's band. In the evening a thunder shower, with distant lightning at night in all quarters of the sky.

Friday, July 23.—To the Imperial Palace—Cabinet of Antiquities—the Treasury—Divine service at the Jewish synagogue—public gardens with Strauss's band. The cameos and intaglios, and the rare and delicate objects of art, some by Benvenuto Cellini, that we saw to-day, were quite wonderful, and the jewels absolutely seemed to realise the enchantments of Aladdin's cave.

Saturday, July 24.—Visited the church of the Jesuits. The guide expected us to be in raptures, but we did not think it nearly so fine a church as that of St. Peter. There is much false ornament about it, and the pillars and several statues are in imitation of marble. But still worse is the painted representation of a dome overhead as you enter the church. The deception is very perfect as long as you keep to the true point of sight, but from other parts of the church the distortion is quite distressing. I afterwards ascended to the highest accessible part of the lofty spire of the cathedral, from whence the view well repays you for the trouble.

Sunday, July 25.—The morning occupied with

preparations for departure. We left Vienna at four in the afternoon by the steam-boat for Presburg.

We did not find the living at Vienna very expensive, and were much pleased with the civility of the people. But I apprehend that Vienna can be justly appreciated only by a winter's residence there. At this time of the year the city is quite deserted by the upper classes. The Italian Opera, too, had closed for the season. We thought the shops very indifferent, and most of the articles, particularly of apparel, extravagantly dear. On the whole, in spite of the wonders of the place, pictures, palaces, churches, and endless treasures, we quitted Vienna without regret. We seemed, we scarcely knew why, to be constantly looking for something further which was never realised. We were glad to escape from the lofty narrow streets into open country and fresher air.

We left Vienna from the landing-place on the banks of the Danube beyond the Prater, where the scene was quite enlivening; the noble river tearing past us; carriages of various descriptions under the trees; friends, that had accompanied friends to the steam-boat, in motion towards the city; whilst on the deck of the vessel there was kissing of hands, waving of handkerchiefs, and stroking of beards (for there were several Turks on board) in token of farewell, a brisk wind and bright sunshine enlivening the whole.

The Danube for several miles below Vienna presents scenery of exactly the same character as for some distance above, and is not very striking. The current is extremely rapid, and is interrupted by numerous islands and shallows, with a channel consequently very intricate. In about an hour and a half from Vienna we came to a range of low sandy cliffs on our right, with some peasants visible on the ridge in their broad-brimmed hats. We arrived at Presburg at about seven in the evening. Hotel (*Drei Linden*) very indifferent.

Presburg has the appearance of being populous, and the women are decidedly pretty. The cabarets were all quite thronged with men drinking and singing. We here first met with the Hungarian language in inscriptions over the shop-doors and inn gateways. The Danube below Presburg is broken up into several branches, and a fine view of the river and neighbouring country is obtained from the ruined palace on the hill. Much might be said of the historical importance of Presburg, but the chief object of a journal is to adhere to what we actually see and can ourselves describe.

Monday, July 26.—At six in the morning we left Presburg for Pesth by the steam-boat. We met on board a young Hungarian gentleman, who was on his way to the university at Pesth, and who spoke English so perfectly that we mistook him for a fellow-countryman, and he seemed pleased at being told so.

At a place called Komorn we took on board a singular and rough specimen of the Hungarian nobility. His appearance was that of a poverty-stricken wayfarer, but our young Hungarian friend told us that he knew him to be noble, and that he consequently had a voice in the election of deputies. He added that there are two classes of noblemen, the magnates and the nobility, who elect the two deputies sent to the Diet by each of the fifty-two counties. The magnates are called occasionally to a separate chamber of their own, in the Diet House at Presburg, by the king in person.

Soon after leaving Presburg we met a very large covered barge struggling upwards against the stream. It was drawn by sixty horses, driven by thirty bargemen, all shouting and cracking their whips. The towing rope was of an immense length. Several other barges, small by comparison, were lashed to the large one. I have no means of estimating its size, but it was much higher out of the water than our steamer, and was by no means inelegant in shape. We were told that these barges occupy six weeks in going *up* the river from Pesth to Vienna, whilst the steamer goes *down* the same distance in seventeen hours.

Between Presburg, and Pesth we passed Komorn, Gran, with its unfinished cathedral, Vissegrad, and Waitzen. The rapidity of the river gradually diminishes below Presburg. We arrived at Pesth at seven in the evening. Hotel (*Queen of England*) good, and close to the Danube, and to the bridge of boats between Pesth and Buda.

Tuesday, July 27.—Visited the old Turkish baths at Buda. They are supplied by a natural hot sulphureous spring, flowing out of the rock of the Blocksberg. Here men and women of the lower classes were bathing together, nearly naked, in the same pool of hot water. Added to this, which was not a very agreeable sight, some had been cupping themselves, and the blood which lay about gave the place the appearance of a slaughter-house. The water was perfectly clear, and for fear of seeming to intrude upon the bathers without an object, I took a large glass of the hot water from its source, and drank a portion of it. The atmosphere of the bath was excessively hot, but not close, nor was there any disagreeable smell.

Afterwards we walked up to the observatory on the summit of the Blocksberg, from whence there is a very fine view of the two towns and the river between them, and the plains of Hungary. Here we saw a great number of fine swallow-tailed butterflies.

We went to the Opera in the evening, and heard Rossini's "Otello" performed by a German company; an excellent box on the principal tier cost us eight shillings. The performance was more than respectable; the Desdemona had a fine voice, but it was she, and not Othello, who "had fallen into the sere and yellow leaf." The third act was judiciously curtailed, a practice which I have often wished was adopted elsewhere.

Wednesday, July 28.—A bright hot sun, with a violent wind at N.N.W. The dust was insufferable, penetrating within doors, and covering every thing.

We took courage, however, and walked over the Bridge of Boats to the opposite heights of Buda, from whence we saw the clouds of dust rising to a great height in the air over the houses of Pesth, and above the church-steeples. Visited the swimming school in the evening.

Thursday, July 29.—At Pesth, in expectation of the arrival of the steam-boat from Semlin. Walked about the Blocksberg and its neighbourhood.

In the evening went to the swimming school, after which I visited the observatory on the summit of the Blocksberg. Professor Mayer was absent, but I was very kindly received by the Docteur Albert de Monte-Dego, the assistant astronomer, and we conversed together in Latin. The astronomical instruments are mounted on piers of porphyry from the mountains near Gran.

Friday, July 30.—At Pesth. Went in the evening to the Opera of "Belisario," translated into the Hungarian language. It was well performed: the tenor was powerful, and but for a coarseness of style he would have been a fine singer. The Hungarian language, as far as we could judge, is very soft, and well adapted for singing.

Saturday, July 31.—Took a long and hot walk about the environs of Pesth. Visited the palace of Count Karoli, which is a very handsome and convenient nobleman's residence. Many Hungarian noblemen, who are well known in England, possess houses in Pesth and Buda.

LINES.

Would'st thou survey a scene as bright
    As may on earth be found,
Ascend the Blocksberg's craggy height
    By star-eyed Science crowned.

Thence with enraptured eye skim o'er
    Th' immeasurable plain,
Teeming for Hungary's lords with store
    Of flocks, and herds, and grain.

Then, turning towards the breezy west,
    Refresh the wearied sight
With vine-clad slopes and wilder hills
    Enrobed in summer light.

Below, white walls and glittering spires,
    Buda, and Pesth, are seen;
And Danube in unbroken flow
    Rolls deep and wide between;

But when the haunts of men are passed,
    Puts forth on either hand
Two mighty arms to compass round
    And water all the land.

And northwards by those floating mills,
    Two islands, side by side,
With greenest thickets wooded o'er,
    Lie stemming Danube's tide,

That runs in narrow course between —
    Then, swift as thought can fly,
I dream of woods and meadows green
    On Thames's banks that lie.

> "O, happy hills! O, pleasing shade!
>   O, fields beloved in vain!
> Where once my careless childhood strayed,
>   A stranger yet to pain."
>
> Return, return! inconstant thoughts;
>   What tricks doth memory play!
> Forbear to mingle scenes like these
>   With others far away.
>
> O Nature! still, where'er I roam,
>   Thee, goddess, I revere;
> Then let me dwell on scenes of home,
>   Less mighty, yet more dear.
>
> He thy best worshipper shall prove
>   Who feels it pleasing pain,
> By leagues of earth and sea removed,
>   To drag the lengthened chain.

Sunday, August 1.—We left Pesth at four in the morning by the steamer for Drenkova. The vessel was crowded with passengers, and the weather very hot. The principal places we passed during the day were Földvar, Tolna, Baia, and Mohacs. Baia in the last year was almost entirely destroyed by fire, but it is rising rapidly from its ashes.

The character of the river is now quite altered: the banks are low, flat, and covered with woods; wild, untrodden, and, apparently, interminable. At Mohacs many of our fellow-passengers left the vessel, which was a great relief to us. We lay down at night upon extemporaneous beds made up in the cabin, and got as much sleep as the tender mercies of the fleas and mosquitoes would allow. We had taken precaution, at Pesth, to manufacture some mosquito-nets of gauze, which we found of the most essential service. The bite of the mosquito is more painful than that of the common gnat, but I do not think it swells so much. A distressing malaria fever is very common on the low marshy wooded banks of the Danube. Pools of stagnant water are left in the swamps by the receding of the winter inundations, which, mixed with large quantities of putrid vegetable matter, make the climate at certain seasons very unhealthy.

Monday, August 2.—On board the steamer. The same endless forests and wild ugly swamps. To-day we passed Vokovar, Illok, and the fortress of Peterwardein, and at night came to Semlin and Belgrade; they are both on the right bank of the Danube, but on opposite banks of the Save, which here falls into it. The Drave also falls into the Danube on the right, above Vokovar, and the Theiss on the left, below Peterwardein. The solitude of the banks of the river was only interrupted occasionally by the appearance of swarthy and savage-looking Hungarian peasants, and their wretched straggling dwellings. Another uncomfortable night on board the steamer.

Tuesday, August 3.—Early in the morning we passed the ruined fortress of Semendria, and at about nine o'clock we entered, near Basiasch, a defile of high sandy hills, partially covered with stunted brushwood, with an eagle or two soaring magnificently over the heights. Further down the character of the hills closely resembled that of the South Downs, near Brighton. Several more eagles soon made their appearance. Next came Moldova and the cave of Golumbacz; and then, passing through a fine defile of the extreme Carpathian mountains, we came to Drenkova at about one o'clock. Here we embarked with our baggage on board a large rowing boat, as we had to pass the rapids, where there is not water enough for a steamer. The river being pretty full of water, the fury of the rapids was not so great as we had expected, and we were a little disappointed with their effect.

Soon after passing the rapids we came to the famous defile of Kazan. The rocks here are of hard limestone, peaked and precipitous, and the admixture of foliage is quite enchanting, heightened as the effect of the whole is by reflections from the surface of the river, which is here pent up and narrow, yet perfectly smooth and tranquil, and, therefore, very deep; a complete contrast to the scene of the rapids above. When we reached the middle of the defile the sun left us, but still illuminated the rocky peaks, thus thrown brilliantly out on the deep azure ground of the sky behind them. The scene so novel, so tranquil, and so lovely, will ever remain in my memory. In the first part of the defile we met six small barges being towed up on the Servian bank by gangs of from ten to twenty Servians, who, wherever it is practicable, walk along the remaining track of Trajan's towing-path, cut in the abrupt face of the rock. We could trace, here and there, for a long distance, the square holes in the

Orsova on the Danube.

rock, that were chiselled out by the Romans, into which beams of wood were inserted supporting a pathway of planks laid upon them and upon the ledge of the rock. Some of our party preferred what we saw to-day to the Wirbel and Strudel; for my own part, I still adhered to the superior magnificence of the river scenery between Linz and Vienna.

Our whole party in the rowing-boat consisted of about twenty-five passengers, several of them Orientals; we were rowed by six men in the bow, and two in the stern; one other acted as steersman. The rowers were wild-looking men, wearing high Dacian sheep-skin caps; they pulled well together, with a paddling stroke, well calculated for a heavy boat, with bad short oars. At about eight at night we arrived at Orsova. Inn (*the Hirsch*).

Wednesday, August 4.—As we had to wait four days for the steamer, we drove over in the afternoon to the Baths of Mehadia. Let no one regret any delay that affords an opportunity of visiting them. Mehadia is about fourteen miles from Orsova; the drive is beautiful all the way, following a clear mountain-stream called the Czerna, which rises in the Carpathians. At a few miles from Orsova, you pass, on the left hand, the ruins of an old Turkish aqueduct close to the road.

Mehadia is beautifully situated in a deep gorge of the Carpathians; it somewhat resembles Matlock, but is on a much larger scale. The surrounding mountains are extremely steep, from about 2000 to perhaps 4000 feet high; and are all, with the exception of a few of the highest, clothed with wood to the very summit. The scenery is quite unlike what I had ever met with before: vastly inferior, indeed, to the Alps in scale, but very pleasing. The crags are tenanted by numbers of eagles which are constantly soaring about. We met on our road with a great number of parties of Austrian infantry on their way to Mehadia, where there are extensive barracks. The rough baggage-wagons drawn by oxen, the irregular march of the men, and the groups refreshing themselves under the trees, were picturesque in the extreme.

When we arrived at Mehadia, the place was full of company, walking up and down, and staring out of the windows, but no one took any notice of us. We drove up to what seemed to be the best-looking house of entertainment; the door stood wide open, people in the dresses of all nations were loitering about, but there was no one that ostensibly belonged to the establishment. We entered, and after perambulating a very extensive passage, and calling about us without success, we at last entered a room where we found a grave-looking personage, with account-books before him, and officials with him, whom we took for the landlord, but he turned out to be the quartermaster; so we made our bow, and ended by obtaining lodgings elsewhere, fortunately in a clean state. All the houses in Mehadia appeared to be in connexion with one another, making up a large nondescript place of accommodation partaking of the nature of inn, boarding-house, bath, and barrack. The house we first entered had been built for troops, but was now let out in lodgings.

Thursday, August 5.—At Mehadia. Very heavy rain with thunder in the morning; afterwards fine and hot; but owing to the rain our beautiful little river Czerna was swollen and muddy. Mehadia is the great place of resort for the higher classes of Hungarians and Wallachians; but the company is of all nations, and the variety of costumes gives the promenade the appearance of a fancy ball. A military band of music plays morning and evening. The faces and costume of the female Wallachian peasants in and about Mehadia are particularly attractive.

Mehadia has some wonderful hot springs of both sulphureous and tasteless water. The hot tasteless spring rushes in a torrent out of the solid rock with a loud noise, and passing by a bathing-house, which it supplies, falls into the Czerna, very sensibly heating it for a considerable distance, from whence some idea may be formed of the great heat of the water at its source. The water from the sulphureous hot springs is received into a long range of bathing-houses, where baths may be taken of various degrees of strength and temperature.

Here is also an extensive public bath for the poor and we saw the men and women nearly naked, bathing together in the same pool of sulphureous water, as at the old Turkish baths at Pesth, except that there was a wooden partition in the water, which separated the men from the women whilst immersed

The length of time they remain in the water is very great; many were lying round the margin of the pool covered up with clothes to encourage perspiration after bathing. Besides these hot springs, Mehadia is abundantly supplied with excellent cold spring water.

Friday, August 6.—Took a long walk about Mehadia. Nothing can exceed the beauty of the innumerable subjects for the pencil that present themselves on all sides. On a tour like ours no one can sufficiently regret not being possessed of the inestimable talent of sketching. We noticed several English pointers about Orsova and Mehadia, probably belonging to Hungarian gentlemen.—Returned to Orsova in the evening.

Saturday, August 7.—Orsova is a military village belonging to the Austrians, on the frontiers of Hungary, Wallachia, and Servia. The environs are interesting, and the view of the Danube and the immediately surrounding hills is extremely beautiful.

In the market at Orsova we saw, for the first time, the sanatory regulations of quarantine in force. The Austrians have a quarantine against both Servians and Wallachians, and the Wallachians a quarantine against the Servians, so that the three nations cannot intermix. Arrangements are therefore made, and rules rigidly enforced, to prevent contact; and bargains are made aloud by the buyers and sellers across a double post and rail, and the goods purchased undergo certain fumigations, and the money that changes hands is passed in a ladle through vinegar by a proper officer.

To-day at Orsova we saw two or three of the Austrian gun-boats which cruise up and down the Danube, Save, and Theiss. They appeared well appointed, and were highly picturesque objects. Along the banks of the Danube, and near Orsova and Mehadia, we saw many of the rude and solitary stations erected for the sentinels of the Austrian military frontier. This *cordon* is maintained by the inhabitants of what are called the military provinces, every one of whom, under a certain age, is bound to serve so many days in the year, in return for grants of land from the government, and thus they are naturally led to mingle agricultural with military occupations. This living boundary was originally instituted as a defence against the incursions of the Turks, and now not only enforces the regulations of the customs and of quarantine, but performs the part of the *antennæ* or *feelers* of government, extended to a distant part of the empire. Their union of military and agricultural habits accounts for the very picturesque and straggling march of the troops we saw between Orsova and Mehadia; yet had occasion required, they would instantly have formed into line with the most soldier-like precision.

Sunday, August 8.—This morning at seven o'clock we bade farewell to Christendom, and were once more launched upon

> "The wandering stream,
> Who loves the Cross, yet to the Crescent's gleam
> Unfolds a willing breast."—WORDSWORTH.

leaving Orsova by the flat-bottomed boat for Cladosnitza, which we reached in about two hours and a half. Just below Orsova is an island upon which stands a Turkish fortress, in a situation, as we thought, ill calculated to resist an attack made upon it from either bank of the river. The passage of the famous rapid called the Iron-gate is about a mile long, with a perpendicular fall, as we were informed, of fifteen feet. The bottom of the river is full of very hard sharp rocks, and the river foams and tosses throughout the whole distance in magnificent style, not without very dangerous whirlpools; a slight error in steering might instantly cause a most serious accident. The scenery of the banks is not remarkable. At Cladosnitza we first set foot on quarantine ground. Here we got on board the steamer that was waiting for us in order to proceed down the river to Czernavoda.

Soon after we reached the remains of the buttresses of the bridge thrown across the Danube by Trajan in a single summer. From what is now seen on Trajan's column at Rome, the road over the arches appears to have been flat, as in our newest bridges.

At Cladosnitza the whole scene on board the steamer assumed a more Oriental character; there were a great many Turkish and Greek passengers, and the sailors were Servians and Bulgarians. The German language was exchanged for Italian. This steamer was cleaner and better appointed than the one in which we came to Drenkova from Pesth. The customary request,

Turks on board the Steamer.

"not to talk to the steersman," was written in English, modern Greek, Turkish, and Arabic.

In about an hour from Cladosnitza we obtained a fine, though distant, view of the Carpathian mountains, and thought we could distinguish snow on some of the heights.

Among our fellow-passengers there were three Jewesses and a very pretty Servian playing at dominoes; the Jewesses wore, strung round their necks and on their head-dresses, a great quantity of Austrian and Turkish gold coins; the Servian wore a Greek dress. They looked at *one* of our party with great interest, and were curious to examine the work she was about. The figures and dresses of the sailors, and the second-class passengers in the fore part of the vessel, amused us very much; several women scalding fowls, an old Turk sitting cross-legged cleaning knives, with other characters to us both new and entertaining.

The range of the Balkan mountains (the ancient Hæmus) then appeared in the distance, and remained in sight until the close of the day, when the sun set over them in great splendour. In the course of the day we saw some flocks of pelicans white as driven snow. At about seven in the evening we arrived at Widdin, and heard, for the first time, the Muezzim's call to evening prayer from the minarets of the mosques. At night the stars shone with great brilliancy, and it was perfectly calm, but by no means sultry; it is, however, on nights like these that the fiend Malaria is abroad;

not riding the tempest, but coming " with wicked dews brushed from unwholesome fens," preceded by his vaunt courier the trumpeter Mosquito.

In a shelf of books in the cabin, designed for the amusement of the passengers, I observed " Sketches by Boz," " The Pickwick Papers," and some of Mrs. Trollope's most popular writings. These works becoming standards of recreation on board a Danube steamer, outdoes Dr. Johnson's finding a volume of his " Rambler" in a cottage in the Hebrides, which he mentions with such exultation in his Tour, as being indeed popularity. Thus ended a novel and interesting day.

Monday, August 9.—Came to the towns of Nicopolis, Sistova, and Rutzchuk; to the latter not until the evening. The outworks and the minarets of Rutzchuk have a fine effect as seen from the river, but on landing the meanness of the streets and houses is almost startling to one who enters a Turkish town for the first time. However it certainly is not so dirty and ill-conditioned as I had heard it represented to be. It is very populous, and not without commercial activity. The Danube is about three miles broad here, and we observed on the river a good class of boat, like that on the Thames about Woolwich; very different from the wretched tubs we had hitherto seen in use. The mosquitoes have all on a sudden ceased to torment us, but we cannot get rid of the fleas. Though touring for pleasure, we have been " made acquainted with strange bedfellows." Just out of the town of Rutzchuk I caught a beautiful sphinx moth, which, with the butterflies on the Blocksberg, are the only insects of any *beauty* that we have met with.

Tuesday, August 10.— At six in the morning the steamer reached Silistria, the capital of Bulgaria, and between ten and eleven o'clock we arrived at Czernavoda.

Czernavoda is a miserable-looking Bulgarian village, and does not afford the slightest accommodation for travellers. The Bulgarian banks of the river are generally rocky, and the neighbouring country wild, open, and arid. The Wallachian side is a dead flat of great extent, and a very unhealthy district. The thermometer stands at 95° in the shade, and this is the temperature we have been subjected to all the way from Orsova. There is a fine breeze blowing all day, but so drying that crumb of bread exposed to it becomes in half an hour as crisp as biscuit. One of our fellow-passengers, an English gentleman, brought out his gun; he allowed me to take a shot with it, and I killed one of the small species of river gull; the bird fell into the stream, and a Bulgarian instantly stripped and plunged in after it. We observed that he struck with his arms as a dog strikes with his fore legs in swimming.

In the meantime the steamer was being unloaded of its heavy baggage, which was packed on small wagons, each drawn by two oxen, and immediately forwarded overland to Kustanjè. Several large falcons were hovering about the rocks, with now and then a flight of storks floating at a great height in the air. Some vultures, too, made their appearance over the brow of the hill, evidently, together with some wolf-like dogs, watching a Bulgarian skinning and cutting up a sheep that had just been killed on the shore. Turkish boys swimming in the Danube, elder Turks performing their ablutions, and engaged in noon-day prayer with their faces turned towards Mecca, with the animated and busy scene of unloading the steamer, all under the beautifully blue sky and splendid sunshine. In the evening we all went on shore, and amused ourselves in various directions with guns, sketch-books, and whatever means we had, or could invent, of passing the time agreeably until dusk, when we returned to our steamer to sleep.

At Czernavoda we bade farewell to the Danube, after a voyage down its stream of about 1200 miles, performed on the wings of steam in twenty-six days, including seven days spent at Vienna, five at Pesth, and four at Orsova, so that we were ten days and nights on board. The Danube is of very nearly the same size as the Ganges, and is the largest river in Europe except the Volga. Its tributaries are not less than an hundred in number, of which a fourth part are navigable rivers. Throughout its whole course, from the Black Forest to the Black Sea, it is distinguished by classical and historical associations, although most of these are of a less peaceful character than might beseem the annals of a river. Above Vienna its banks present the most beautiful and varied scenery imaginable; and there is something in the very rapidity of the stream, and the overpowering succession of objects during the first two days of the downward voyage from Ratisbon, that fills the mind with an agreeable perplexity, as if a lovely vision had passed away, upon which it was delightful to dwell. Below Vienna the interest in no respect falls off, and the scenes which at intervals present themselves are among the most striking to be found in Europe, replete with subject-matter and imagery for the artist and poet. There is also a gloomy grandeur, and a peculiar sublimity in the vast solitary tracts of swamp and forest on the banks of this mighty river; regions ceded by man to the dominion of marsh exhalations, and to the mosquito, who says, "My name is Legion."

Wednesday, August 11.—Early in the morning I took a farewell swim in the Danube, and at six o'clock we left Czernavoda for Kustenjè, in light carriages, each drawn by four horses, driven by a postilion. The luggage had been forwarded overnight by one of the bullock-wains. Czernavoda is rather more than forty miles from Kustenjè, and we went the whole distance with the same horses, stopping three times, twice for a very few minutes, and once for an hour and a half. The whole journey was performed in less than seven hours, including the stoppages. The horses were small and active, and were driven at a gallop nearly all the way. They did not appear to suffer in the least from the pace, or from the heat of the sun, and arrived quite fresh at Kustenjè.

There was no regularly made road, and our route lay over an undulating prairie country, such as I had never seen before, frequently without a bush or a tree within sight. The soil was light and sandy, with coarse grass, thistles, and brushwood. We noticed a great quantity of different sorts of birds; vultures, large hawks, storks, and some birds not unlike partridges; and on some swampy, unhealthy-looking lakes which we passed there were multitudes of pelicans, beautifully white in the morning sun, with wild ducks, geese, coots, bitterns, and herons, and great quantities of the common plover. We also passed by the sites of two or three Bulgarian villages that had been destroyed by the Russians, marked only by the rude tomb-stones of the unfortunate inhabitants. There were also in the plain some large herds of the common buffalo, which are here in very general use as beasts of draught, and troops of horses running wild.

One of the lakes that we passed by was very striking. It was backed by low grey limestone cliffs, and was nearly covered over with weed of a bright reddish-brown colour, but in one corner or bay the surface of the water lay smooth as a mirror, and reflected the blue sunny sky with amazing brilliancy, whilst the banks were surrounded with large patches of

Journey from Czernavoda to Kustenjè.

tall reeds of a vivid green. We overtook the baggage-wains that had left Czernavoda the previous evening about ten miles from Kustenjè, at which place we arrived early in the afternoon.

Kustenjè is finely situated on a small promontory overlooking the Black Sea; it was once a flourishing town, but is now in a very ruined state, having been nearly destroyed by the Russians. It boasts of some antiquity; fragments of marble columns and rich remains of Roman structures are met with among the ruins, and the sound of its ancient name, Constantina, still lurks in its modern appellation.

The house we went to afforded much better accommodation than we had expected. It belongs to the Danube Steam Company, who rebuilt it, and fitted it up in a humble way for the accommodation of their passengers. There were two regular beds, but we all, chiefly for fear of the insects, preferred sleeping on the simple divans or sofas belonging to the rooms, and passed the night with very tolerable comfort. Mr. Marenovitch, the Company's agent, who came with us from Czernavoda, presided over all the arrangements with the greatest civility and attention.

The route by land from Czernavoda to Kustenjè has been only recently adopted by the Company. The alternative is to persevere from Czernavoda down the Danube to Galatz, and there to get on board another steamer which goes by the Soulineh mouth of the Danube into the Black Sea, and so to Constantinople; but the journey is now shortened by 200 miles, and exposure to the mosquitoes and the unwholesome swamps of Galacz is avoided.

Several of our party, as well as myself, were here attacked by low fever and great depression, but we recovered in a day or two. I am happy to say that G——'s health and spirits never suffered in the least.

Thursday, August 12.—The Ferdinand steamer from Constantinople having arrived in the night, we looked forward towards speedily getting away from Kustenjè. However, we were alarmed by a report that news having arrived of the occurrence of a case of plague at Constantinople, from whence our vessel had just arrived, the Kustenjè authorities would not allow the steamer to take us on board, as that implied communication with the shore. Mr. Marenovitch, however, managed to overrule this difficulty, and we embarked once more, for the last time before reaching Constantinople. Had we not succeeded in embarking from Kustenjè, we should have had to retrace our steps by land to Czernavoda, and re-embark on board the steamer we left there, and so proceed to Galacz, and wait there in great discomfort until the Ferdinand could have come round to meet us by the mouth of the river. On the whole we had fine weather for our voyage, but there was enough wind to make the vessel roll a great deal, to the practical illustration of Byron's well-known couplet respecting the billows of the Euxine.

Friday, August 13.—At about ten o'clock in the morning we quitted "the vast encincture of that gloomy sea," and entered the Bosphorus, passing the classical Symplegades on our right.

The charms of the scenery of the Bosphorus cannot easily be exaggerated. Hills, forts, towers, and villages, appear in succession, whilst its bays and windings endow it with the several beauties of river, lake, and sea. The water is of transparent purity, and of the most beautiful azure colour. A large shoal of porpoises accompanied us for several miles, gambolling and leaping into the air from wave to wave, and we could distinctly see them when darting along beneath the surface, though the water was far from being smooth. Nothing could be more delightful than our transition from a tumbling sea to the swift current of this beautiful strait, that bore us down through scenes so novel, so interesting, and so intrinsically beautiful, to a city equally celebrated in ancient and modern times.

The minarets of Constantinople now came in sight, and much sooner than we expected we found ourselves at anchor in the Golden Horn. Just as we arrived, the Sultan was embarking to cross the Bosphorus, on his way to a mosque on the Asiatic side, it being Friday, the Moslem Sabbath. The officers of state accompanied him in their caiques: it was a gorgeous and animated spectacle; and the thunders of the salutes from the ships of war, gaily decked out with ensigns and streamers, seemed to bid us welcome to the waters of the Bosphorus, and to the full enjoyment of the celebrated view of the Imperial city, or rather three cities in one; Constantinople and the Seraglio point on our right, Pera on our left, with Scutari on the Asiatic side; palaces, mosques, and their minarets; cypress-trees, towers, and shipping; sky, water, and sunshine, all blending and harmonising together.

In due course of time we left our steamer, and transferring ourselves and baggage to the light caiques of the Turkish boatmen, we landed, and walked over a pavement, that must be seen and felt to be imagined, up the apparently interminable ascent of Pera, and along its principal street to the Hotel (*Belle Vue*), where we established ourselves very much to our satisfaction.

But something ludicrous is very apt to intrude itself upon the most charming illusions. We were sitting in all the pride and freshness of our arrival in an Eastern city, enjoying the brilliant evening and the view of Constantinople, thinking that every sight and sound must be equally new, when suddenly we were regaled by the popular air of "*Jenny Jones,*" with several others of the same class, most sonorously played on the key-bugle; at intervals we heard loud voices, and the *English Shibboleth* so plainly pronounced as to satisfy us of what nation the musician and his companions were.

We had now been travelling and seeing new places for exactly seven weeks, without having experienced any serious fatigue, and with scarcely an hour's indisposition; and, I trust, upon that evening we did not hear with indifference the voices of the Muezzims calling all the city to prayer.

Saturday, August 14.— Walked about the hot, steep, and cruelly paved streets of Pera and Galata. The town, now that the weather is dry, is very tolerably clean; thanks also to the dogs, hawks, and vultures, who are the scavengers of the place; and although the heat is great, yet there is throughout the day an agreeable air from the Bosphorus. We were rowed about in the evening in caiques, and walked home after we were set on shore, making a little round by the cemetery of Pera.

Sunday, August 15.—In the morning crossed over to Constantinople to visit the slave-market. The slaves that are exposed here for sale are chiefly black females, who are bought by the Turkish ladies as household servants. They are generally well treated, and suffer no ills but those which all servitude is heir to. We noticed a few white women, and a few black boys, to be disposed of. We walked round the market under a covered way, and saw through lattices a great many slaves in rooms set apart for their reception. Some were already equipped with the Turkish dress, and seemed to have the liberty allowed them of walking in and out of the apartment. They did not appear at all unhappy. They looked very attentively at G——, and, as we passed by, they smiled and seemed to have their joke among themselves. There were, however, in the middle of the market some wretched-looking meagre objects, lately arrived from Nubia, leaning against the walls half asleep in the sun, or squatting on the ground, ridding one another of vermin. They had nothing but the coarsest possible drapery of sackcloth thrown over them, and yet they contrived to wear it not ungracefully.

From thence we walked by the Mosques of Sultan Achmet and of St. Sophia, and visited the obelisks and Brazen Column in the Atmeidan. We returned home to Pera, and I took a Turkish bath, which I found extremely agreeable.

You undress leisurely on a sofa, in a cool airy part of the building, and a blue cotton cloth is wrapped round your middle so as to form a sort of petticoat; you are then conducted into a room, the atmosphere of which is very hot, without being close or stifling: water hot and cold is supplied from marble fountains, and runs in channels along the stone floor; here you remain, and the perspiration soon runs off the skin in large drops: if you can bear it you are conducted from hence into an apartment still hotter, and shortly an attendant arrives who throws a bowl or two of water over you from the marble fountain, and then proceeds to lather you from head to foot with soft soap, at the same time gently rubbing and kneading the joints and muscles. After this you are again rinsed thoroughly with water, and are reconducted to your sofa, where you are carefully dried, wiped, and kneaded as before, and are left covered up, with a cloth wrapped round your head, turban-fashion. Here you remain half an hour or more in a delicious and tranquil reverie, to enjoy a pipe if you choose it, and inhale the fresh air of the apartment, and drink iced lemonade or sherbet; this may sound as if it were a dangerous process, but it is the received custom to do so, and I suppose it allays beneficially the ferment raised in the circulation by the bath. The process throughout is agreeable, and leaves no subsequent lassitude, but rather confers a sensation of power to resist the heat of the climate.

After dinner we walked to the cemetery of Pera, and enjoyed a most lovely view of the Bosphorus. On one side was the setting sun, and in the opposite quarter of the sky a dark storm of rain that cast a deep purple blush over the water, throwing a large ship of war as she lay at anchor out into bold relief: fine dusky hills on the Asiatic side, with the faint outline of Olympus in the distance.

Monday, August 16.—Received a visit from Mr. Cartwright, the English consul. In the afternoon in caiques to Scutari on the Asiatic side of the Bosphorus.

Scutari is a large and ancient town, though considered as a sort of suburb of Constantinople: the principal street is wider than any we have yet seen in Constantinople or Pera, and the mosques and public fountains are beautiful; the cemetery is held in great veneration by the Turks; it is very extensive, and adorned with vast groves of large and antique cypress-trees.

In the course of our walk we bought some excellent sweetmeats at a confectioner's shop, and seeing a pretty little girl of about seven years old standing by,

I offered her some, but she looked at me very gravely as if I had affronted her, and ran away half frightened. There were quantities of the most delicious grapes for sale in the streets, and we bought a large basket full, but it was evident that we were not looked upon as desirable customers. It is generally observed that the inhabitants of Scutari do not take much pains to conceal their dislike of the Franks.

The current of the Bosphorus is always strong, and when we returned the wind freshened. This afforded us an opportunity of seeing how admirably the Turkish boatmen manage their caiques. They use sculls very much overhanded, and when there are two or more scullers, they pull powerfully and well together. The caiques are most elegantly formed, very light, with sides rather high out of the water. The sitters recline in the bottom, in order that the weight may be kept as low as possible. When first set afloat in one, you are tempted to exclaim with the Bard,

> "And now I have a little boat,
> In shape a very crescent moon!"

It is quite surprising how in windy weather they ride over the swell of the Bosphorus, and when it is calm with what ease and rapidity they glide along. The Golden Horn, in particular, is throughout the day enlivened with hundreds of them of all descriptions in motion in every direction, from the caique of the poor boatman whose fare across is half a piastre, to the private caique of the rich Turk, decked out with golden-fringed scarlet or blue draperies, and the rowers in their full-sleeved shirts and Greek caps, and the Pasha himself, with his chibouk, reclining majestically in the stern.

Tuesday, August 17.—We went shares with another party of English in the expense of a Firman, by virtue of which we gained admittance to the Mosques, and to the Seraglio palace, the Sultan being now resident at one of his summer palaces on the Bosphorus. The Seraglio, at a very rough guess, stands upon not less than fifty acres of ground, and I have heard its circuit estimated at three miles. From without you are agreeably bewildered by the domes and minarets, and the whole style of the architecture mingling so beautifully with the noble cypress-trees; but when within the courts, or inside the apartments, you are occupied chiefly by the general idea of great spaciousness, rather than by any particular attractions that they offer, and are not sorry to look out of the windows upon the lovely prospects of the Bosphorus which they command.

In many of the rooms there was a profusion of really handsome gilding; but the Turkish customs do not admit of the European style of furniture, and from the nakedness of the apartments I thought it very likely that many such articles as rich carpets and ottomans are removed from palace to palace with the court. In one immense room we saw a very small table in bad French taste, and a few of the common French artificial bouquets under glass shades.

But the arrangement of the bath-rooms, with their fountains and pavements of marble, was quite delicious. The few attendants that we saw about the palace were in their ugly modern dress, and looked dirty and ill-conditioned. The gardens are not extensive, but are beautiful, and well watered, and contain many plants growing in the open air, which in England are seen only in hot-houses. Works of art, pictures, and statues, are not to be met with in the Seraglio, but perhaps it is a relief now and then to visit a palace that does not possess them. It is the general effect produced by the whole, aided by blue water, sky, and sunshine, that repays you for the exertions of the day.

We then were indulged with a sight of the interior of the great Mosque of St. Sophia, of that called the little St. Sophia, and of the Mosques of Sultan Ahmed, and of Sultan Solyman; but on entering we were obliged to take off our shoes, and put on thin slippers, or walk barefoot. We were agreeably surprised by their magnificent dimensions, and their fine general barbaric effect. The interior of the dome of St. Sophia is fifteen feet wider across than the dome of St. Paul's, and is one mass of gilt mosaic work; and its exterior is surmounted by a magnificent gilt crescent, the dimensions of which I have heard very variously stated. The other mosques are not quite so large, but are, perhaps, as well worth seeing from their unmixed style of oriental architecture. Innumerable silver lamps and ostriches' eggs are suspended from the domes of them all. No detailed description of these truly wonderful edifices could be kept within any reasonable bounds. It was just the hour of noon when we entered St. Sophia, and as soon as the voice of the Muezzim (himself unseen) rang with thrilling power through the entire building, all the true believers present prostrated themselves to the earth. I never witnessed a more striking spectacle. We brought away with us some broken pieces of the mosaic work of the roof, which were offered to us for a few piastres.

In the Mosque of Sultan Ahmed we saw a kind of reading school for young lads, who were being educated, as we were informed, as Imaums or priests. They were reading the Koran out loud, in concert with their teacher, in a noisy, chanting, irreverent tone. When they concluded, all that were present rose up except one, a strange-looking figure, who persisted in remaining with his book open before him, which they at length took away from him, and he then got up and stalked away with the self-important gestures of insanity. He was described to us as a wandering Dervish, and reputed mad, which greatly enhanced his sanctity. Before quitting the Mosque we saw a Frenchman, who was of our party, carelessly spit upon the pavement; we immediately called his attention to what he had done, for had the Turks observed it, we should probably all have got into trouble, and he would certainly have been most severely punished. I mention this circumstance because there will be occasion to allude to it again.

I then hurried back to Pera to see the Mewlewli

or Dancing Dervishes. The meeting was held in a place of worship of their own, with a kind of circus in the midst, with a very smooth floor. I counted fourteen Dervishes prostrate round the circle; the chief knelt on his carpet opposite the entrance, and was engaged audibly in prayer, to which the rest from time to time made responses. The chief had on a skyeblue robe, and a thick felt cap of a light brown colour, in the shape of a truncated cone, bound round with a green scarf. The rest wore the high cap without any decoration, and long robes of dark hues. When the chief made an end of his prayer, a Dervish in the gallery began a very loud chant, whilst the whole company, headed by the chief, paraded twice or thrice round the room, with their arms crossed upon their breasts, the inferior brethren making profound obeisances as they passed the carpet on which their chief had been seated. Then began a low wild melancholy strain, without any distinct melody, but not unpleasing, performed on a flageolet and flute; this continued for about ten minutes. The Dervishes then once more prostrated themselves with their faces to the earth. A small drum then sounded, upon which the Dervishes rose up and let fall their outward robes, appearing in short white jackets, and long white coarse petticoats that trailed on the floor; their feet were bare. The music then struck up again, accompanied by a loud noisy chant, and every Dervish, except the chief and one other, who acted some intermediate part, began a slow, solemn, rotatory movement, or dance, with their arms held out horizontally, their revolutions throwing

Dancing Dervishes.

out the white petticoat into a conical shape, with the border steadily floating a few inches above the floor. This continued without intermission for a quarter of an hour: the Dervishes then ceased their revolutions and repeated the obeisances, and then once more resumed the dance for another quarter of an hour, accompanied by the music and song as before. The ceremony closed with a dying fall in the music pleasingly managed, and before the last devotees had ceased to turn round, the friction of the bare feet upon the floor was plainly heard. There is something almost touching in the quiet and composed demeanour of the chief and his followers; and the entire absence of any appearance of fatigue or giddiness on the part of the performers in this extraordinary ceremony is quite surprising.

Wednesday, August 18.—In caiques to Therapia, to visit Mr. and Mrs. Bankhead. In the afternoon we crossed the Bosphorus from thence, and ascended the hill called the Giant's Mountain, from whence the view is really superb. You look one way to the Black Sea, and in the opposite direction down the windings of the Bosphorus to the Sea of Marmora, with Olympus in the distance. We returned to Therapia to our friends, and slept that night at the little inn.

Thursday, August 19.—Bathed in the Bosphorus. Walked and rode about Therapia and its neighbourhood: the scenery is beautiful at every turn: slept a second night at the inn.

Friday, August 20.—Returned by water to Pera from Therapia; the wind blew fresh and there was more sea than was agreeable in a caique. On our way to Pera we stopped at the Sweet Waters, a delightful place of public resort on the Asiatic side of the Bosphorus. Here we saw a great many arabas or carriages, profusely gilt, drawn by oxen or horses, with richly ornamented harness; they were filled with women and children. We caught glimpses of some very pretty faces among the women, who for the benefit of the air had loosened the asmacks of white muslin which usually envelope their necks and faces, but we were quickly warned off to a respectful distance by the guard. The children were very pretty, with dark eyes and hair, and handsomely dressed in a costume peculiarly becoming to childhood.

Some of the Turkish ladies got out of their carriages and walked about; others sate still eating sweetmeats or fruit, or taking coffee; one elderly lady I saw enjoying her pipe very comfortably. The feridjeè, or loose cloak, conceal their figures entirely. G—— and her maid went amongst them, and they asked her all manner of questions in a sort of *lingua Franca*, and wished to see her take off her bonnet, and begged her to take the front combs out of her hair. Though as inquisitive as children, they were gracious and ladylike, and offered her coffee and whatever they had with them; they were waited upon as usual by black female slaves.

A Turkish Araba.

There were besides several family groups enjoying themselves under the trees, seated upon their bright coloured carpets, with their yellow slippers ranged in order round. There were also several Turks of rank on beautifully caparisoned Arabians, with boys on ponies; asses for hire with scarlet housings, conjurors, vendors of fruit, lemonade, sherbet, water, and sweetmeats; every thing, in short, that the description of place was likely to afford, but new and interesting to us. To complete the picture, the shore was lined with the caiques of the company, assembled from various parts of the Bosphorus, with their gaily dressed rowers lying on their oars.

Saturday, August 21.—Mr. L—— F—— very unwell. Went to the leather Bazar in Constantinople, and from thence to the madhouse, which is divided into two spacious courtyards: in the first we were shewn, much to our surprise, some wild beasts in large dark dens, by way, I suppose, of preparing us for what we were soon to see; accordingly in the next court we saw the patients, about twelve in number, all confined by very strong iron chains and collars round their necks; their cells were large, but neither paved nor floored, and seemed as if they must be very cold at night, even in summer. They were all more or less clothed, though rudely enough, and their persons were not wholly neglected. One poor wretch who was about to undergo a washing was a pitiable spectacle; he was quite naked, with the iron chain and collar still about his neck, and his body disfigured with bites of vermin; and as he sat on the ground in this condition, with his bare shaven head, he was no inapt representative of Job in his affliction. We noticed but one very noisy patient. There was an Arab patient with only a rough blanket thrown over him, sitting in the furthest window of his cell, with the sun streaming in through the bars over his dark features, laughing and conversing with a visitor; such a study for a painter I scarcely ever saw before. Two others in opposite parts of the same cell had been smoking, and were now throwing their cherry-stick pipes at one another; another, whose arm was bound up as if severely injured, had, as they told us, twice broken his chain. We were given to understand, I know not how truly, that it was permitted to irritate the patients to frenzy, as though their ravings were oracular, and the effect of divine inspiration. Any one within the court had free access to the cells and to the patients. We were rather surprised at not feeling more shocked at a spectacle which we should probably have shuddered at had we heard it described as we saw it. Possibly the preconceived idea of happiness or of misery generally outstrips the reality.

We continued our walk to the desolate site of the barracks of the exterminated Janissaries; the whole quarter is in a most ruinous condition; we there saw a beautiful marble fountain quite dried up and disfigured; the truest emblem of desolation. We then came to a single column apparently of late architecture, with the Roman eagle at each of the four corners of the Capital. From thence we made our way to the Historical Column, or, as it is sometimes called, the Column of Honorius and Arcadius; the base alone is standing, and is in a very ruinous condition: the column fell down about 1716, two years before Lady M. W. Montague came to Constantinople. We ascended the remaining steps of the winding staircase which once, I conclude, conducted to the summit of the column, and found a small chamber withinside the base. The whole seems to have been constructed of white marble; some of the blocks were extremely large; we measured one of them in a very rough way, and estimated its bulk at about 200 cubic feet; there were other larger blocks, but out of our reach.

Sunday, August 22.—In the afternoon we went in a caique to the Sweet Waters of Europe, on the banks of the river Lycus which runs into the Golden Horn. There was a very high wind, and we quarrelled with our boatman, and found no company when we arrived. Here there is a pretty summer kiosk belonging to the Sultan.

Monday, August 23. — Made purchases in the bazars, and dined in Constantinople on kabob, which is a genuine Turkish dish, and very good; it consists of mutton cut into small pieces, broiled on skewers, and served up on large flat cakes resembling crumpets. On our return we saw the smoke of a fire in a distant part of the city, and saw the fire-signal hanging from the Seraskier's tower.

Tuesday, August 24.—L——- F—— rather better.

Called on Mr. Hanson, the banker. Took another Turkish bath. Dancing Dervishes again at two o'clock.

Wednesday, August 25.—Rode with F—— to see the old walls of Constantinople; it is a curious and interesting round to take, with some fine points of view. On our way thither we passed under the Aqueduct of Valens, which is a stupendous work, and still conveys water; but without the assistance of natural scenery, aqueducts are rarely beautiful objects.

In the course of our ride we saw several hoopoes, birds which I never before saw on wing: they are frequently sold in the streets as articles of food. Soon afterwards we passed by the smoking ruins of above an hundred houses that had been destroyed by the fire last Monday; however, this is but a small number for a Turkish fire to consume.

As we returned we met a Greek funeral. The corpse was carried on an open bier, strewed with flowers, and its face exposed. The Bible was laid upon its breast. Two boys followed with lighted candles, with priests, friends, and mourners, chanting a dirge. We rode home by the Bazars, and crossed the Golden Horn by the bridge of boats, and so through the cemetery to Pera.

Thursday, August 26.—Grand review at Scutari. This review, we were informed, was the first that had taken place in the present Sultan's reign, and the second only since the adoption of the European military systems and dress. There were about 8000 troops reviewed; light and heavy cavalry and artillery, and large columns of infantry. The light cavalry regiment of lancers looked well in a body; and the red Fez or bonnet with its deep blue tassel, and the red pennon of the lance above, presented, when viewed in a mass, a surface tinted like the flower of the cactus. Individually, men, arms, and accoutrements were very shabby. There were no scabbards to the bayonets, and much cannot be said of the manœuvring of the troops. The artillery practice, however, was very creditable. The review took place on a fine tract of undulating open country with mountains in the distance: the sea of Marmora, the Bosphorus, Constantinople, and the cypress-crowned cemeteries of Scutari filling up the view. The Sultan, preceded by a guard, and the officers of his household, came on the ground in an odd, but picturesque carriage, with a body of the shape of a sedan chair, richly gilt, with a crimson hammer-cloth, and drawn by four beautiful white horses. He was followed by his mother, and the foreign ministers, in carriages, and by the chief officers of state superbly mounted on Arabians. We obtained a very good view of the Sultan's features: he is much marked with the small-pox, but has fine dark eyes.

Here were also several very handsome arabas filled with the women of the imperial harem, but they were closely veiled, and the guard kept all spectators at a respectful distance. The arabas were drawn by white oxen of great size and beauty, with handsome frontlets, and long bent pieces of wood curved backwards from their yokes, to which the tails of the animals were attached with pendant bells, tassels, and ribands.

Presently we heard a report that a Frank had got into a dispute with the Turks, and that he had been severely beaten, and dragged to Scutari as a prisoner, between two horse-soldiers, and that in all probability he would undergo the bastinado. The account had been, as usual, exaggerated; but it was true that he had been beaten, and he kept his bed in consequence for some days. One of our party went to visit him, and he proved to be the very Frenchman who had accompanied us to the mosques, and who spat upon the sacred pavement. We never heard the origin of the quarrel on the day of the review; but it is clear that a man who could commit so gross an inadvertency as he did on one occasion, might be supposed to have acted not very wisely on another. On our return we bought another basket of the delicious grapes of Scutari.

Friday, August 27.—Saw the Sultan go to Mosque on horseback, attended by the grand vizier and officers of state. We then, by a short cut, got up the hill before the cavalcade, to a place where the road wound round the ascent, and again secured a good position together with several Turks who had petitions to present, which were all received in order by the appointed officer as the Sultan passed by. The Sultan's saddle-horses, of which several were led, and those of his officers, were of the greatest beauty.

Saturday, August 28.—Again to the slave-market, which had a livelier appearance than when we visited it before. The greater part of the slaves were black females. We saw some miserable-looking objects amongst the black little girls, and one black lad quite naked was being rubbed in the hot sun all over with oil, which gave him a most attractive polish. But we were delighted to see some dishes of hot potatoes and garlic, which a man was carrying on his head, upset in the crowd, and the little hungry black wretches scrambling for them. This place, notwithstanding the dirt of it, abounds, like every other corner of Constantinople, with interesting studies for painters.

We then went to look round us once more in the Bazars, and whilst there we heard the report of " Fire in Pera!" Upon this we lost no time in making the best of our way homewards, together with a crowd of Jews, Armenians, and others, who closed their shops in the Bazars, and hurried away to save their property in their dwelling-houses. We got across the water in the midst of unusual bustle, and rushed up the hill of Pera, which is not the pleasantest or easiest ground in the world to hurry over. We found that the fire was not far from our hotel, but that it was being rapidly got under. I saw one small brass fire-engine which could scarcely be of any service hurried along through the crowd on men's shoulders towards the scene of action. But the brigade of firemen wore workmanlike dark dresses, and were armed with powerful axes, and very long poles with iron hooks and spikes at the end, intended to be used if necessary in pulling down the houses adjoining the fire, so as to smother it in rubbish.

However, it was soon extinguished, and when all alarm had subsided, we re-crossed the water to the Bazars; but on our way home we again heard the report of "Fire!"—this time at Constantinople. But happening to call on our way home at a perfumer's with whom we had had some bargainings in the early part of the day, we found him hastily shutting up his shop and hurrying off to the scene of the conflagration, which was near his residence, just as we had ourselves hurried away to Pera in the morning. This was quite in the spirit of the lines—

> "Fire on the quarter-deck,
> Fire on the bow;
> Fire in the main-top,
> Fire down below!"

Sunday, August 29.—Dancing Dervishes at their convent at Cassim Pasha. I went rather in expectation of some ceremony different from that which I had already witnessed at Pera, but was disappointed. I here saw a very little boy, quite a child, running about in the dress of a Dervish. The high conical cap gave him a most ludicrous appearance. When the ceremony began, the poor child went through the prostrations and reverences exactly with the rest. But I was glad to see that he soon grew tired, and put on his slippers, and went out to play with others of his own age.

In the afternoon we rode round by the bridge of boats to the aqueduct of Valens, and to the walls as before, and outside the city to the suburb of Eyoub. Eyoub or Job, the standard-bearer of Mahomet, was killed by the Saracens, and buried there. Hence Eyoub is considered by the Turks as a most sacred place of burial; here, also, is their most sacred mosque, where the Sultans are inaugurated by girding on the sword of Othman. The Turks do not much like the Franks to approach the place. The cemeteries here are kept in good order, and the tombs are covered with ivy and creepers under the shade of lofty trees. We then ascended the hill, and obtained a superb view of Constantinople and the Golden Horn. We rode from thence along the brow of the hill looking down upon the European Sweet Waters, and in a valley near the Sultan's kiosk, saw an encampment of Turkish artillery, to which we descended, and then crossed the hills to Pera.

Monday, August 30.—To Therapia a second time. In the afternoon with Colonel H—— to the gigantic plane trees in the Sultan's Valley, the Valley of Roses, and the village of Buyukdéré. Dined and slept at Therapia.

Tuesday, August 31.—From Therapia to the aqueducts by Belgrade and Purgos, and to Justinian's aqueduct, and so home to Pera, making a ride of about thirty miles through an interesting country. We first ascended the valley of Buyukdéré, and enjoyed the beautiful prospect as we looked back upon the Bosphorus from the great arch of Sultan Mahmoud's new aqueduct between Buyukdéré and Bagdsche Koï. On arriving at Belgrade we saw the whole system of collecting water in large reservoirs or bends, as they are called, for the use of Pera and Constantinople. The forest of Belgrade is the only wooded region near Constantinople; the thick shades, and the damp atmosphere hanging about the trees, is considered a great protection to the reservoirs, and on this account the wood is never cut, which probably is the cause why Belgrade is at certain seasons extremely unhealthy, and subject to malaria fever. Two out of the seven aqueducts we remarked were curved.

On arriving at Justinian's aqueduct we halted for an hour under the shade of its immense structure, and examined it in every accessible part, and climbed up the hill forming one side of the valley across which the aqueduct was built. On the summit, where the stone was broken away, we obtained a sight of the stream of water conveyed by it, which was two feet deep, and two feet across, but the channel was only half full; the water was running with considerable rapidity. Underneath the shade of one of the arches were two wild-looking shepherds, with sheep, cows, and goats. The goats were scrambling about the stonework in the most picturesque manner possible. There were a few fine butterflies in the forest of Belgrade, and during our ride we saw several hoopoes, and caught a tortoise, and met a long string of camels laden with charcoal; and on a large open piece of ground we saw thousands of a small animal of the weasel kind that burrowed under ground as we approached. Waterwheels were in general use for irrigating the cultivated lands.

Wednesday, September 1.—Quiet morning at home. Rode in the afternoon.

Thursday, September 2.—Quiet morning. At two o'clock to the ceremony of the Howling Dervishes at Scutari. The preliminary prayers and prostrations somewhat resembled those of the Dancing Dervishes, but with this difference, that incense was made use of, and the accompanying song had a slight resemblance to what I have heard in Roman Catholic services. These Howlers do not wear a dress peculiar to themselves as the Dancers do, but appeared as if they formed a secret society consisting of all professions. We observed one of the Dancing Dervishes standing in a composed attitude amongst the chiefs of the Howlers. After some long prayers and hideously noisy responses, the devotees, at least fifty in number, stood up in a row quite close together, and began to recite the words "Lă-ăllāh-ĭl-allāh!" bowing themselves alternately backwards and forwards, keeping time to their recitative. This motion and the repetition of the words became gradually more and more rapid, with occasional violent ejaculations of "Hu!" whilst the noisy chant and responses in a yet shriller key were kept up without cessation by two others who remained kneeling on the floor. The movements and vociferations gradually assumed a more frantic character; the agitations of the devotees, and, I am shocked to add, of several children who bore their part in the ceremony, became dreadful. The heads of some were tossed about so violently that their features were scarcely distinguishable, and their limbs quivered with excitement, whilst they uttered the strangest guttural noises, mixed with some extremely fine deep bass notes which were heard at intervals in the storm of vociferation. But at a signal from the chief who presided over the whole, they reseated themselves round the room with the utmost composure; some few, indeed, wiped the sweat from their brows, but not one appeared exhausted or even out of breath.

A pause now ensued, during which the Dancing Dervish, who had hitherto remained a quiet spectator, came forward, and revolved in the middle of the circle by himself for several minutes. Then the Howlers re-arranged themselves, and recommenced their movements; this time from side to side instead of backwards and forwards, with their recitative as before, but changing the accentuation of the syllables from Anapæstic, as it were, to Iambic,—" Lă-ī-lăh-īl-lăh-lāh ! " However, in this second act of the performance the noise again became stunning, and the contortions and apparent excitement of the Dervishes soon reached its climax, the poor children bearing a part as before, when the whole ended quite suddenly at a signal from the chief, and the devotees quietly resumed what outer garments they had laid aside, and walked away.

The whole was little better than a revolting and obscene sight. All these Howlers were low ruffianly-looking fellows; there were several blacks and several soldiers among them. They are tolerated by the

Howling Dervish.—Scutari.

government, but have had their ceremonies modified and cut down by the late Sultan. They are generally considered as impostors, and altogether bear but indifferent characters, and are not respected as much as the Mewlewlis or Dancers. Round the room were suspended various iron instruments with which the Howlers used to maim and torture themselves, but such exhibitions have been forbidden by authority. Our impression was, that had they indulged in such pastimes, we should rather have felt inclined to halloo them on like fighting dogs or beasts in a ring, wholly undeserving of sympathy. The exhibition lasted two hours.

Friday, September 3.—In the morning to the Bazars. Quiet afternoon.

Saturday, September 4.—Some of our party to Therapia, and others to the Bazars. I walked with M—— to the site of the Hall of Justice, a large space covered with ruins, the courts having been all destroyed by fire. Thence we went to the great cistern of Constantine, which is underground, and contains a vast body of water. It is constructed inside with very handsome arches and pillars, and did not convey the idea of having been originally intended as a cistern. It was impossible for us to see the whole extent of it. I understand that its Turkish name signifies " The Thousand and One Pillars." We then passed by the Burnt Column, as it is called, but we had seen it before, more than once, in the course of our rambles.

Sunday, September 5.—Divine service at the Chapel of the Embassy. Quiet afternoon.

Monday, September 6.—Some of our party again to the Bazars. Preparations for departure.

Tuesday, September 7.—At five o'clock in the afternoon we left Constantinople by the French steamer for Malta.

Thus we passed twenty-four entire days at Constantinople, and without making any excursion to a greater distance than Therapia or Belgrade, we were actively employed during the whole of the time. With the exception of the interior of the mosques, we thought that the chief attractions of Constantinople lay out of doors, in the exquisite views of the hill-enthroned city and the Bosphorus obtained on every side. Above the general mass of the houses rise the spreading cupolas, relieved so happily by the lofty and glittering minarets, which, not without an elegance all their own, partake of the gracefulness both of the spire and of the mast of a ship. These, together with the dark cypress trees, the clear blue Bosphorus, and its light caiques, the ever-busy scene, the gay harmony of lively colours, the sky, sunshine, and fresh breeze, are the chief ingredients in the picture, a combination perhaps unequalled in any other part of the world. Happy are they who possess the talent of drawing! Not only the general features of Constantinople, but the shipping, the boatmen, the porters under their enormous burdens, the beggars, the vendors of a thousand different articles, are subjects for the pencil, on the water and on the land, all equally admirable.

The Turks are certainly not without natural refinement of manner, but I do not imagine that much insight into their true character can be obtained, or that any thing can be learnt concerning their domestic economy except after long residence in the country, or through opportunities afforded only to a few. I have heard, however, from high authority in such matters, that a dinner at a Pasha's table is really excellent.

It is a drawback at Constantinople that there are no public places of entertainment: all acquaintance with the people must be picked up in the day-time in the streets and Bazars. Neither is it very safe to go out after dark. The troops of dogs without homes or masters that are seen in every street during the day, generally asleep in the sun, towards dusk give themselves the rousing shake, and begin to shew their wakefulness by barking at every Frank they meet. At night they prowl about the city, and would probably, especially in the winter time, attack any one that fell in their way. Besides, whoever is found in the streets at night without a lantern, is forthwith consigned to the Guard-house.

The goods in the Bazars are set out in very tempting array. They are so arranged that one Bazar is appropriated to the sale of arms, another to the sale of drugs, a third to leather slippers, a fourth to horse-furniture, and so on for furs, jewellery, silks, embroidery, &c. The motley crowd, exhibiting the dresses of all nations, and made up of all ranks, degrees, and callings, and the brilliant and varied colours of many of the articles exposed for sale, seen in long perspective, with the arched roof of the building high over all, by a light subdued just sufficiently to take off the glare, form a scene that a painter might succeed in expressing on canvass, but of which words cannot convey an adequate idea. I need not add that the sellers reap a tolerably plentiful harvest from the European customers. The bargaining, without which no purchase is ever completed, is often very amusing; half or a third part of the original demand is usually taken with the greatest composure.

It is absolutely necessary in Constantinople to walk a great deal, and to be equal to a little fatigue. There are no wheeled carriages excepting the arabas, which only go a foot's pace, and to which most of the streets are inaccessible. Nor is riding on horseback always convenient. However, very good horses are to be procured when required for more distant excursions. They gallop well, and are remarkably sure-footed in steep and slippery places.

In a merely amateur and sketchy excursion like ours, we must in a city like Constantinople have passed over a thousand points important to be studied and understood. Much, however, that is perhaps of value, and certainly much that is very pleasing, will remain indelibly fixed in our recollections, serving at the same time to feed and cherish one predominant feeling of thankfulness that England is our home.

Wednesday, September 8.—On board the steamer. At about eight o'clock in the morning, passing Gallipoli and Lampsacus, we entered the Hellespont, which is by no means equal in beauty to the Bosphorus; it has been not inaptly compared to the Menai strait. It is needless to advert to the innumerable associations connected with this classical region. We then came to the castles of Roumelia and Anatolia, which we feel reluctant to call by any other names than Sestos and Abydos, though they do not occupy the sites of those ancient towns, of which but very scanty traces remain. Modern Abydos is a pretty large town. The strait is a full mile across in this part, with a rapid current, and the European and Asiatic castles will probably always be looked upon as determining points, and serve as starting places for future swimmers adventuring for love or glory. Why have we not yet heard of an *Etonian* performing the feat of swimming across the Hellespont?

We then came in sight of Imbros, with Samothrace beyond it. These islands are very mountainous, and resemble in outline Snowdon and the Carnarvonshire hills; and soon afterwards we arrived off the coast of Troy, with Ida not far inland.

. . . . . "Classemque sub ipsâ
Antandro, et Phrygiæ molimur montibus Idæ."
Æn. III. 5.

The region of the supposed site of Troy, as seen from the deck of a vessel, is wild, woody, and very hilly. Next, " est in conspectu Tenedos," then the craggy point of Cape Baba on the left, and Lesbos with its mountain scenery on the right, and we remarked some very high ground far inland in Asia Minor. Superb starlight at night, with the sea in a state of beautiful phosphorescence.

Thursday, September 9.—Early in the morning we found ourselves at anchor in the bay of Smyrna, which is very large, and surrounded by mountains, with abrupt volcanic outlines. We went on shore, and having eaten some kabob, and drunk some coffee, with a chibouk of excellent tobacco, we made some trifling purchases, and continued our walk through the scene of devastation occasioned by the late fire. We then walked up the hill at the back of the town through the burial grounds and their ancient groves of magnificent cypresses, to visit the extensive ruins of the Castle, or Acropolis, and the site of the ancient Christian church of Smyrna. Eastward you have a grand view of the town, the bay, and the surrounding heights, and westward of the little river Meles, with its green wooded banks, and of the neighbouring country and high mountains beyond. The tradition is, that Homer was born at Smyrna or near the river Meles, whence Tibullus calls the poems of Homer " Meleteæ Chartæ."

Towards the right as you look down upon Smyrna the bay runs up into a narrow salt-water marshy creek, that meets a beautifully green, and apparently highly cultivated tract, lying between the steep hills, which, however, has all the appearance of being a chosen abode of malaria. But close on its borders on either side, and just on the rise of the hills, lie the villages of Bougea and Bournabat, which are much resorted to as rural retreats by the people of Smyrna, and by the resident English merchants, several of whom we met riding home in the evening, dressed in white jackets, and with gay-looking pack-saddles of Persian carpet behind them. By the bird's-eye view of Smyrna from the summit of the hill, we were enabled to compare the space occupied by the ruins with the remainder of the town, and to calculate that rather more than a third of the whole had been destroyed by the fire. The ruins were not blackened, but, on the contrary, were whiter than the rest of the town; for the dark brown roofs were gone, and the interior walls were exposed to the light, and the rubbish that lay about was chiefly plaster, forming a harsh and melancholy contrast with the verdure of the surrounding orchards and garden-grounds.

The fury of the flames must have continued unabated to the last, for the extreme houses to the northwards on the barren hill-side were entirely destroyed, so that the fire had literally nothing further to devour; but it seemed to have wreaked its expiring fury upon two unfortunate cypress-trees, which, though nearly two hundred yards beyond the last houses, were quite shrivelled up to the top, and the hill, nearly two

E

months after the fire, was still covered with shreds and remnants of burnt bedding and furniture that had been carried thither for safety, but which caught fire, and were consumed where they lay. Several trees that had stood in the midst of the conflagration were more or less injured. Its rapidity must have been very great, for we saw the stem of a large vine against the wall of one of the burnt houses quite charred on one side, whilst the side next the wall was not even discoloured. Every thing opposed to the flames built of stone or marble remained standing. We saw the streets in the course of rebuilding in the old way, without any precautions against the recurrence of so sweeping a disaster.

Both here and at Constantinople there were oil-jars quite large enough to contain a man who wished to make one his hiding-place. This was a real commentary upon the stratagem resorted to in the story of the " Forty Thieves," which was such a puzzle to us in our childish days.

Remarked a very pretty little fair-haired Jewess about twelve years old, gracefully dressed, and with a quantity of gold coins strung about her neck, drawing water at a fountain with a very elegantly shaped pitcher. We could not avoid contrasting her in our own minds with the figure of an English cottage girl performing a similar office, but to the disparagement of neither of the two.

As it was the fruit season, we saw a great number of long strings of camels laden with grapes and figs, and passed through whole lines of delicious melons piled up for sale. Singular appearance of the crowd of long-necked camels in the narrow streets. Returned to our steamer at night to sleep.

Friday, September 10.—We went again on shore and purchased a few more trifles. Some fresh passengers came on board, and with them some friends, who remained until the vessel got under weigh. One young lady at the hour of parting went down the side crying bitterly, and continued sobbing hysterically in the boat that was rowing her away, though it was no more than a *sister's* white handkerchief and lily hand that waved after her from the deck. A stout portly merchant in an ample white waistcoat was attended by a good-looking young Turk, who, when it was time to part, threw himself in tears into the merchant's arms. We remained occupied with the beauties of the bay of Smyrna until we approached " Scio's rocky Isle," over which we saw the sun set.

Saturday, September 11.—Early in the morning we arrived at the island of Syra, where the old town is built upon a very steep conical hill. Here our two companions, L—— F—— and F——, left us to perform their quarantine, intending to go on to Athens. Having taken on board some passengers from Alexandria, we weighed anchor from Syra about noon, with a distant view of Delos, hard and fast where it was left by its tutelary deity between Gyaros and Mycone. The weather was delightful. At night we saw a great deal of vivid lightning in the horizon, with bright starlight overhead, whilst the sea round the vessel was most beautifully phosphorescent.

Sunday, September 12.—Cape Matapan and the Island of Cerigo; afterwards sea and sky, with enough swell to discompose bad sailors.

Monday, September 13.—At sea. At one time we thought the weather rather threatening, but towards the afternoon the wind died away, and in the evening it fell perfectly calm. The phosphorescence of the sea at night was quite lovely.

Tuesday, September 14.—Sea as smooth as a mirror. At about ten o'clock in the morning we reached Malta, and passing by the mouth of the great harbour, the bristling batteries, and the lighthouse of St. Elmo, cast anchor immediately in the Quarantine Harbour, and were consigned, twenty-five in number, some of us to Fort Manoel, and others to the Lazaretto. The greater part of the day was taken up with our arrangements in Fort Manoel, preparatory to spending eighteen mortal days in that delectable retreat. We hired a servant to wait upon our own party, now consisting of ourselves, V——, and M——, who accompanied us in the steamer from Constantinople. Our furniture was supplied at a fixed rate per day, and our meals in the same manner, from establishments attached to the Lazaretto. We were delighted with receiving intelligence that the Vanguard was in harbour. We immediately sent off word to A——, informing him of our arrival; he sent an answer in surprise and joy, and did not fail to pay us a visit at the *Parlatorio* as soon as possible.

Wednesday, September 15.—In Fort Manoel.

Thursday, September 16.—In Fort Manoel.

Friday, September 17.—In Fort Manoel.

Saturday, September 18.—In Fort Manoel.

Sunday, September 19.—In Fort Manoel.

Monday, September 20.—In Fort Manoel.

Tuesday, September 21.—In Fort Manoel. Our amusements in quarantine were necessarily very limited, and it will easily be imagined that the whole artillery of the Fort was directed against the common enemy—Time. Our resources consisted chiefly of bathing in the morning, breakfast, writing letters or journals, sleeping, sketching, which can be pursued even in a lazaretto by the possessors of that precious talent, singing, guitar and flute-playing, dinner (the great event of the day), smoking, which, *in a Pickwickian sense*, was *board* and *lodging* to us, and, if it had been *washing* too, it would have been all the better; with the occasional variety of intercepting the determined march of the ants through our rooms, hunting the lizards basking in the sun, listening to the ponderous knell flung from the belfry of St. John's Cathedral, gazing listlessly at the kites flown from the flat roofs of Valletta flashing white in the sunshine, or at the " ships slowly sinking in the sleepy sea;" then came the report of the evening gun at sunset, when the whole court-yard usually began to re-echo with the recital of the prayers of some devout Mussulman, unseen by day, but now heard in earnest; and next with some popular melody sent forth from British lungs for our entertainment during our evening walk of meditation on the ramparts. Then, as it grew late, having gazed alternately at the brilliant stars above, and the boatmen's lights beneath gliding softly over the water, we retired for the night. Thus were our days passed in Fort Manoel, until the sickness of our companions supplied us with further and more anxious occupation.

Wednesday, September 22.—Two of our immediate neighbours and fellow-prisoners very ill. They were visited to-day by two priests from Valletta, and M——, who has been ailing for some time, was seized with a bleeding at the nose which lasted nearly three hours.

Thursday, September 23.—M—— rather better, but one of our two neighbours appears to be sinking rapidly.

Friday, September 14.—This morning one of our neighbours died, and his companion remains in a very dangerous state. Two others are complaining of illness, but not seriously.

In the afternoon we observed a large carrion crow hovering over the Fort, and finally over that part of the building in which the unfortunate man died. The corpse was laid out on the ground-floor, and the doors and windows were open, but the walls were very thick, and nothing could have been seen from the outside.

The occurrence forced itself upon my notice from its similarity to one that took place some years ago in my own family, and probably there are few who cannot call to mind some circumstances of a like nature brought more or less home to themselves — some similar apparitions of birds at the time of the decease of persons well known and perhaps dear to them. The wonder is, what force of instinct or perception can bring birds wholly undomesticated, and accustomed to range the open air and fields for their food, to the house, or to the very windows of the chamber of death; for, agreeably to the experiments of Audubon the naturalist, birds of prey are guided to their food by the sight alone, and not by smell, a conclusion which tends to throw an air of solemn mystery over these visitations. In the course of the day I mentioned the circumstance to several persons of different nations in Fort Manoel. They had all noticed the bird as an unusual sight in that place, and, without pretending to offer any regular explanation of the phenomenon, they one and all connected the presence of the crow with that of the dead body.

It is no doubt from occurrences like these, and the natural desire to account for them, that the belief has arisen that the souls of the dead inhabit the form of birds, a creed for which we need not travel far from home. See Note 43d to Lord Byron's "Bride of Abydos," and the instances there quoted.

Saturday, September 25.—M—— rather better. An oppressive sirocco wind has been blowing for the last two or three days. The quantity of moisture which the wind deposits is quite extraordinary. As soon as the sun gets low a clamminess becomes perceptible, and a linen jacket is soon wetted through. On clear calm nights, with a north wind, I have not been able to perceive any dew whatever, nor was there any sensation of chilliness or dampness to drive us within doors. Some interesting results would probably be obtained from experiments made at Malta with Daniel's hygrometer.

Sunday, September 26.—Sirocco still blowing. M—— not so well.

Monday, September 27.—The sirocco wind changed to north: guardianos playing at dominoes out on the ramparts by moonlight.

Tuesday, September 28.—We have now a medical man in quarantine with us to attend upon M——: brilliant moonlight.

Wednesday, September 29.—M—— a little better in the morning, but worse again at night.

Thursday, September 30.—M—— the same: the companion of our neighbour who died is said to be recovering. Mrs. B—— called upon us and saw M——, but he rambled and did not know her.

Friday, October 1.—This morning we obtained Pratique, and bade adieu to Fort Manoel. Our first care was to get M—— up, he dressed himself, but was evidently in a delirious state; he was taken to Mr. B——'s house. We then went to Durnsford's Hotel in the Strada Reale, Valletta, and found it comfortable and clean. Valletta is a very pretty town: nearly all the houses are of stone, spacious, and well built; the fortifications are most extensive, and are probably impregnable. We visited St. John's Cathedral, and admired the silver plate and the mosaic of the pavement very much, but the gilding is rather heavy, and the roof wants height. The celebrated picture by Caravaggio, of the beheading of St. John, is ill placed and requires more light.

Saturday, October 2.—The faldette, or black silk hood, worn by the women here, is very peculiar; it is certainly becoming, and admirably adapted for every nice shade and gradation of coquetry; it reminded me of the graundee described in the imaginative romance of " Peter Wilkins." Saw some specimens of the Maltese stone-work and silver filigree ornaments, and walked round to see the great harbour from the height of the Barracca.

Sunday, October 3.—Rode to St. Antonio, where we saw the Governor's palace and gardens; the Emir Beschir, Prince of Lebanon, lived there when under the English escort. The ex-Bey of Bengasi is now resident in Valletta, on the Pietà.

In the evening Floriana gardens and band: we afterwards saw a religious procession pass through the streets, accompanied by a crowd of ragged boys, whose devotion or amusement consisted in catching in the hollow of their hands the drippings of the holy wax that fell from the lighted flambeaux.

Monday, October 4. — Visited the magnificent

library of the Knights of Malta, and saw there several specimens of antique Roman pottery; and the stone idols, sacrificial vessels, and fragments of Phœnician pottery found at Hagiar-Keem, near Crendi, and an unique sarcophagus in terra cotta, found in a tomb on the Benjemma hills. We then took a calèche and went to Crendi, about seven miles from Valletta, passing through the casals of Lucca and Micabba, where we noticed the beauty of some of the carved stone balconies, and the size and external architecture of the churches. The ruins at Crendi are supposed to be Phœnician, and it is probable that further numerous vestiges may yet be discovered in their neighbourhood. Two temples have been excavated; the one nearest the sea is the most perfect. In their general character they reminded me of Stonehenge, but they exhibited a more distinct plan, with traces of architecture and sculpture of a decidedly Hindoo character; the stone idols that were found near the altar, are very like what are called Chinese Josses, except that they are, without exception, female figures; and it is remarkable that all the heads are wanting, which, by the construction of the necks of the idols, evidently might have been attached and removed at pleasure, and small holes are seen which some kind of fastenings for the heads originally passed through. The altar, which remains in perfect preservation, is dotted with holes, as are also many stones throughout the building, and on each of its four sides it is ornamented with palm-trees in relief springing from a basket. Some of the fragments of the pottery are also dotted with holes; others have small cylindrical nodules worked in relief upon them, and others have their surfaces wrought into a representation of scales. Judging from the curves of some of these fragments, the entire vessels must have been of a very large size.

Tuesday, October 5.—At Valletta: bought some of the delicate Maltese lace mittens. Diodorus says of the Maltese, " Variorum operum artifices habent, inter quos excellunt qui lintea *insigni subtilitate* ac mollitie texunt."

Wednesday, October 6.—M—— still very ill. This morning we visited the Monte di Pietà, a government institution for advancing money on pledges. It is admirably regulated, and every thing seemed in the best possible order. Some old-fashioned jewellery and silver ornaments which were shewn to us were really curious.

In the afternoon we rode over to the deserted Citta Vecchia, which was the capital of the island before the arrival of the Knights of St. John in 1530. We visited the Cathedral, St. Paul's Church, St. Paul's Cave, and the Catacombs, which are very extensive and of high antiquity; some fragments of Roman pottery were exhibited to us, as well as several Egyptian and Phœnician idols found in the neighbourhood, which would have greatly surprised us had we not seen the ruins at Crendi, and the idols discovered there. In continuation of the passage quoted above,

Diodorus says of Melita or Citta Vecchia, "Domus illic sunt perpulchræ, suggrundiis et albario opere magnificenter exornatæ."

Thursday, October 7.—Rode on horseback in the country round Valletta. The agricultural instruments at Malta are very primitive: the soil is extremely light, or rather by nature there is none, but whatever can be obtained for the purpose is industriously scraped together, and thus arable fields are actually constructed, and are fenced in with stone walls, frequently, where the ground is uneven, in terraces one above the other. The cactus plant is a silent but ceaseless assistant labourer in the process of improving the soil, insinuating its roots into the fissures of the rock, and thus hastening its pulverisation. The threshing-floor is merely a smooth space cleared out on the barren surface of the rock, where the corn is trodden out by oxen, on which occasion, as I was told, the animals are muzzled. The forks are ingeniously made entirely of wood; a single piece is cloven in two places, so as to form three prongs, which are kept separate by wedges, and the whole is held compactly together by strong pegs. The harrows are of heavy wood, but small, and without teeth. The plough is very simple, and resembles that described by Virgil in the first Georgic, but is adapted only for very light soils; in fact, the share itself is frequently merely of wood. In ploughing, an ox or a cow is generally yoked with an ass, but the Maltese asses are powerful

MALTA.

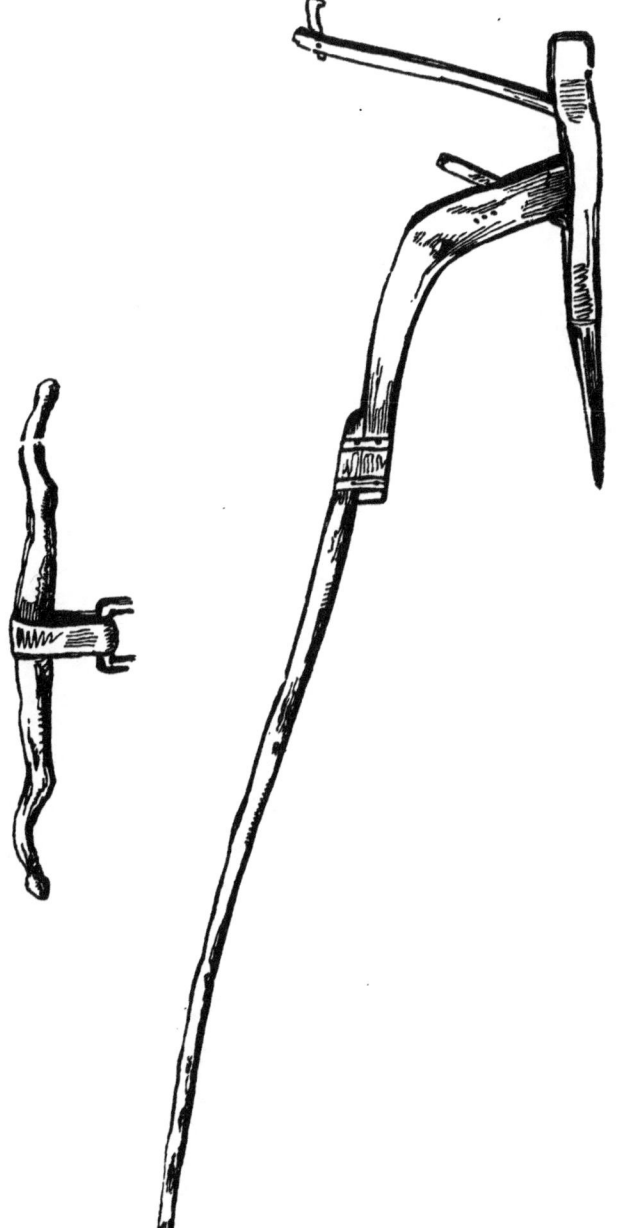

"Continuo in sylvis magnâ vi flexa domatur
In burim, et curvi formam accipit ulmus aratri;
Huic à stirpe pedes temo protentus in octo:
    *   *   *   *
Cæditur et tilia antè jugo levis, altaque fagus,
Stivaque, quæ currus à tergo torqueat imos."—GEORG. I. 169.

animals, so that the two are pretty equally matched. The ploughman guides his plough with the left hand, and in the right carries a staff, furnished with a rude whip-lash, and shod with iron at the other end, which serves the purpose of cleansing the ploughshare. At a small farm near Valletta there were some remarkably fine heifers, the produce of a cross between English and Sicilian cattle, that would have shewn well at an English agricultural meeting; they were fine examples of Virgil's

"Longo nullus lateri modus."

Cotton is grown in Malta in considerable quantities, and of a peculiarly fine quality. Many a picturesque group of female peasants is seen at work upon it from the very pod. It appears from Cicero that in his time the Maltese were celebrated for their manufacture of cotton cloth. The cactus opuntia, Indian fig, or prickly pear, grows in every part of the island; the fruit is rather insipid, but very refreshing, and of all colours; there are also a few bananas and palms; the carubba or locust-tree is not uncommon; it bears a pod resembling the tamarind in appearance and taste, which is eaten by the peasants, and is frequently given to horses and cattle. Some contend that St. John was fed in the wilderness with the fruit of the *carubba* and wild honey, and not with the *insect* called the locust. Oranges are produced in abundance; the blood-red variety, I was told, derives its colour from an admixture of pomegranate blood by grafting.

These productions shew that the heat of the climate is very great. The name of Malta, or Melita, tempts one to suppose that the island must once have been celebrated for its honey.

Friday, October 8.—Saw a very fine specimen of the ass of Gozo belonging to an English officer quartered here; the animal stood nearly fifteen hands high, and was equal to almost any weight. I got upon him, but he was not pleasant to ride, being very low before, and possessing a mouth upon which all indications were thrown away. But the general appearance of power about the animal was very striking, and the enormous ears not turning " with motion dull upon the pivot of his scull," but moving quickly like those of a well-bred horse, together with its large bright eyes, gave to its head a peculiar and startling animation. It had been the winner at the races in the island, and in consequence the good-humoured owner has been honoured with the title of " Primo Somaro" ever since.

In the evening rode ronnd Borgo, Senglea, and Victorioso, on the side of the harbour opposite to Valletta. M—— worse.

Sirocco: when this wind has been blowing during the night, the streets early in the morning are as wet as if there had been a heavy shower, and throughout the day the dampness adheres to the pavement that is in shadow, and is deposited afresh on that which the sun from hour to hour ceases to shine upon.

The effects of the black sirocco, described as bringing a dull haze mixed with fine sand from the shores of Africa, we did not experience.

Saturday, October 9.—At Valletta: quiet day.

Sunday, October 10.—Floriana Gardens and band.

Monday, October 11.—Rode to the Boschetto, where there is a garden and an abundant spring of fine water. An extremely large stalactite, brought from the Island of Gozo, is set up as a pillar in front of the spring.

Tuesday, October 12.—Visited the armoury in the palace at Valletta; the chief curiosities were a sword and pistol combined in one weapon, a Turkish air-gun, and a cannon taken at the siege of Rhodes, made of copper tube, bound round with rope and cemented over. In the afternoon rode round the casals of Nasciar and Mousta, and visited the immense church lately commenced at the latter place, the walls of which had been raised round about the old church, which they completely enclosed; two lofty towers were completed, but the roof was not yet begun, and the dome of the old church rose to sight above the encincture of the new walls. It does not appear that there are any funds forthcoming at all adequate to the support of such an undertaking, which is necessarily carried on by labour voluntarily contributed in the shape of a religious exercise, or imposed as a penance. The inhabitants of all the casals take a superstitious pride in their churches, but at

Mousta they have carried this feeling to a length palpably absurd.

We saw many female faces at the little square unglazed windows, like those in the pictures of Murillo; and many a study for a *Rebecca* among the peasant girls carrying water on their heads in classically shaped pitchers; the poor inhabitants are compelled to undergo this additional labour if their dwellings lie far from the line of the aqueduct. This noble work runs directly across a great part of the island, and was constructed by the grand master Vignacourt.

Wednesday, October 13.—On board the Vanguard with A——; she is a splendid eighty-gun ship on Sir W. Symons's model. Invited some friends to tea in the evening.

Thursday, October 14.—Poor M—— much worse: rode with A—— to Entahleb, which is really a spot very well worth visiting; there is a fine sea-view as you approach it, and it is one of the few places in Malta where foliage and verdure are to be met with. The cliffs, with the chapel and cottage above, are relieved by orange and pomegranate trees, with cultivated patches of garden below; a most agreeable change from the arid rock we had ridden over, well-nigh calcined by the excessive heat of the sun.

Friday, October 15.—We left Malta at night by the Mongibello steamer for Naples. Our poor friend M—— remains with Mr. B—— in a dangerous state.

Malta is certainly a very interesting island, but the extreme heat and intense glare are serious drawbacks upon it as a residence; yet it is far from unhealthy. The Maltese are a singular race, and the mixture of languages spoken in Valletta is very diverting; they are superstitious, but industrous and surprisingly active. They have all dark hair and dark black eyes, with a peculiar national cast of countenance and an expression not very agreeable: even among the women we did not remark much beauty. Malta is an instance of the superior importance of situation, which more than counterbalances the disadvantages of its climate, soil, and scarcity of water. Owing to its central position and the excellence of its harbours, it was inhabited by the earliest commercial nations, which the relics of antiquity sufficiently shew; from which period to the present it has continued to be a place of importance and a favourite station for shipping. St. Paul, after remaining three months, "departed in a ship of Alexandria that had wintered in the isle," and Cicero says of it "ubi piratæ fere quotannis hiemare soleant." Its modern importance is quite manifest without further remark. The English society in Valletta is decidedly of a high order; we were much gratified by the kind attentions shewn to us by many agreeable families. It is certainly, at first, delightful to think that in December and January, whilst the inhabitants of London are enveloped in fogs and gloom, you may here saunter in an orange garden under a clear warm sky, and gather the ripe fruit hanging over your head; but the variety of amusements afforded by the vicissitudes of our own northern climate is infinitely preferable to any delights that Malta can produce.

Saturday, October 6.—Having passed the " altas cautes, projectaque saxa Pachyni," descriptive to this day of Cape Passaro, and the " præpingue solum stagnantis Helori," early in the morning we arrived at Syracuse. The white summit of Etna was shining in the distance above a stratum of cloud. We landed, and lost no time in setting off for the antiquities, and crossed over at once from Ortygia to the sites of the ancient quarters of the city, Neapolis, Tyche, and Acradina. Passing two remaining columns of the Temple of Ceres, we came to the cemetery, where the ornamental entablatures of the tombs, and a vast number of square niches, are hewn out in the face of the solid rock. Our guide selected the handsomest, and informed us it was the tomb of Archimedes; but it had not the appearance of the tomb of a philosopher, and was nothing like the " columellam non multum e dumis eminentem," described by Cicero. From thence we made our way circuitously through part of Tyche to the upper part of Neapolis, where the remains of the Theatre, which was not built, but hewn entirely out of the side of the hill in the solid rock, detained us for some time. The seats were in tolerable preservation, and so formed as to present a kind of ledge carefully rounded off, and sufficiently raised to prevent the feet of any spectator from annoying the one who sat below him. The staircases were still accessible, though much fallen to decay; the orchestra was partly overgrown with bulrushes and brambles. The water of the aqueduct from Tyche above, after turning some mills, formed a cascade amongst the ruins. Hard by was the Nymphæum or grotto, with its clear cool water, and its deep shade; and in full enjoyment of the fresh breeze, and the gentler influence of the sun, after the heats of Malta, we reposed with pleasure in this interesting spot, with part of Acradina, the Mediterranean, Ortygia, the great harbour, and the tract watered by the Anapus, full in our view. The peculiar enchantment of this spot gradually unsettles the belief that it once stood in the heart of a populous and mighty city; that here resounded the music of the orchestra, and the shouts of a gay or factious audience; that here flashed the expressions of courtly wit; here was a loose given to ruder jests; here were assignations whispered; here political opinions advanced;—for the whole is lying as it were in the lap of Nature; the silence is unbroken save by the dashing of waters, the song of birds, or the hum of insects; the heron takes wing from the rushes hard by, and the lizard basks undisturbed at our feet. If those things were so, here has been regeneration, not decay; for the waters of the city aqueducts have returned to rivulets of the hill; the very seats have been moulded into gradations which the waterfall covers with its spray, and the rainbow comes in glorious stillness into the very centre of the theatre. But this inscription—this regularly fashioned curve—this and that evidence of human design, are things palpable and unanswerable that force themselves upon us, which, however, we would not willingly be rid of; for they impart no touch of melancholy now, but rather modify than disturb the illusion, and place the whole before us as less under the influence of a destroying power than subject to the gentle handling of one which is gradually moulding it into a renewed condition of existence.

Again, here might we sit, with eyes half shut, in a midsummer day-dream, and inwardly rebuild and re-people those deserted regions, remuster the hostile forces of Nicias or Marcellus, and man or destroy at will invading armaments; or cover the pestiferous regions of the Anapus with the bodies of the besiegers, and shape the gaunt spectre of malaria hovering over her unburied thousands, and scourging in fiend-like mercy the proud Himilco home to his native Carthage, there to perish by his own hand; or summon the intendant Verres before us — Verres, the false, the lascivious, the avaricious, the cruel, the sacrilegious—summon him and his lewd band of associates—embody and set forth his piles of plate, his gold, his statues, and his purple. But suddenly the air grows eloquent—breathes and burns with the denunciations of intellect and justice fulminated against the evil-doer. And see, the tyrant flies! *Now* no one fears him—no one values his favour—no one *ever* loved him! He flies, to hide his head in voluntary and miserable exile, there, in an hour of awful retribution, to be stripped and murdered by a spoiler stronger than he.

Having indulged awhile in similar speculations, we left this spot to visit a Roman amphitheatre in good preservation, partly hewn out of the rock, and partly built with large stones, and near that a spacious vaulted chamber half under ground, supported by pillars, something resembling a miniature of the great cistern of the Thousand and One Pillars at Constantinople, though it contained no water.

The enormous excavations called the Latomies, or stone quarries, which furnished building materials for all Syracuse, are not far from the Theatre. These vast pits, whose perpendicular sides are on an average one hundred feet high, lie open to the air and light, but communicate with two or three remarkable caverns. The roof of one of these was supported by rude columns of rock, apparently left for the purpose by the original excavators; in another there was room, light, and shelter, for the operations of a rope-walk; and another is conceived to be the passage of the famous Ear of Dionysius. This latter cavern is fifty feet high, or more, running with a slight sinuosity into the solid rock in the perpendicular side of the quarry; the roof is vaulted, and the sides are slightly curved, so that a section of the cave from top to bottom might be likened to that of a church-bell. The water from the ancient aqueduct above trickles continually down the face of the rock at the entrance of this cave which is beautifully overgrown with the Capillus Veneris.

The slightest sounds made or uttered within are reverberated in an extraordinary though confused manner; but we put no faith in the legend that exhibits Dionysius in the character of an eavesdropper, nor in the received account that this cavern was originally hewn out as a prison, though it may have been used as such; we rather were inclined to regard it as a natural cavern discovered by the excavators of the original quarry, and upon which they afterwards expended some labour, considering it to be of a fine shape, and the secret dwelling-place of a mysterious echo; and in fact we saw in other Latomies which we visited in the course of the day two caverns quite similar to the one in question. It was in one of these hollow and roofless quarries that the three thousand Athenian prisoners were confined at the defeat of Nicias, and, according to the affecting narrative of Thucydides, underwent all the horrors of disease arising from exposure to the heats of the day, and the cold damps at night, superadded to the pains of filth, hunger, and thirst, and captivity in a foreign land. Their sickness, thus arising chiefly from want of covering, was, no doubt, a species of malaria, possibly not unlike that which was so fatal to the Carthaginians when encamped near the marshes of the Anapus, yet which, at the same time, spared the Syracusans: for the soldiers of the besieging army were living necessarily in tents, and exposed in a great degree to every kind of atmospheric change, whilst the Syracusans were separated by the city-wall not only from the beleaguering army, but also from the fury of the pestilence, with the additional protection of the general mass of building. All the observations upon this insidious disease tend to shew that in malarious seasons and districts health is more easily preserved in the closest and most crowded quarters of a city than in an open and airy situation, such as we should choose in England.

The Latomies present innumerable specimens of the fruitfulness of the climate; they are deliciously watered both by the ancient aqueducts and by natural springs; and crags, such as a savage pencil would delight to dash in, are mellowed down by time, and blend their weather-stains with the hues of cool green retreats where Loves, Graces, and Bacchanals, might be drawn disporting. Here are found in profusion the orange-tree, the lemon, the vine, and the fig; noble bay-trees, worthy of a station in a forest, the healing palma Christi, the elegant styrax, the cactus, varieties of the acacia, the graceful amaranthus, and the feathering banana; whilst the steep sides of the quarry, robed in dark ivy, and the light and lovely Capillus Veneris, close in the prospect, thus apparently enriched with half the treasures of the vegetable world.

The Catacombs are situated in Acradina, and on our way thither we passed over a desolate space, where imperfect vestiges alone told of the departed city. Here and there the rock was deeply indented with the tracks of carriage-wheels, and was mapped out, as it were, into the foundations of houses, of which the very stones have ceased to be. These subterranean sepulchres are of prodigious extent, and of the highest antiquity; the cells intended for infants, and those for grown-up persons, are by no means larger than would be required in these days; and there is a total absence of ornament, except that some Pagan and Christian symbols intermingled are distinguishable on the walls in fresco-painting of the rudest kind, indicative, no doubt, of the ages of persecution when the early Christians took refuge in these dens and caves of the earth. The Catacombs lie under the Chapel of St. John, but their immediate entrance is by the subterranean Church of St. Marcian, reputed the earliest place of Christian worship in Europe.

We passed from thence to the Capucine convent, where we had yet to see the largest of the Latomies. It is laid out as the garden of the convent, and richly stocked with vines and fruit-trees; out of it runs one of the caverns before alluded to, resembling the passage of the ear of Dionysius. The monks received us very hospitably, and treated us with cake and excellent wine, which was most acceptable after our exertions. We then rode back to Ortygia along the shores of the lesser harbour, and I made a drawing of a plough at work in a field in Acradina.

Later in the day we visited the Temple of Minerva, which was converted into a Christian church in the

SYRACUSE.

twelfth century; to effect which, and to gain room, arches have been opened in the interior wall, and the spaces between the exterior columns walled up, to the destruction of the symmetry of the ancient fane; but, had not this been done, the probability is that little or nothing of it would have been now remaining; and there is something consoling, and even sublime, in the idea that it has been a place of daily worship during 2500 years.

The once sacred Fountain of Arethusa is in a sadly degraded state. Its situation with respect to the sea accords precisely with the description given by Cicero, but the spring must surely be far less abundant now than it was in his time. The well-known and beautiful fiction is given in the following lines of Virgil, which recognise as the river Alpheus the powerful spring of fresh water said to be still visible in calm weather as it rises from the bottom of Syracuse Harbour.

> " Sicanio prætenta sinu jacet insula contra
> Plemmyrium undosum; nomen dixere priores
> Ortygiam. Alpheum fama est huc Elidis amnem
> Occultas egisse vias subter mare, qui nunc
> Ore, Arethusa, tuo, Siculis confunditur undis.
> Jussi numina magna loci veneramur," &c.
>   ÆNEID III. 692.

But these deities we found had been long since metamorphosed into barelegged washerwomen.

We did not visit the Anapus and Cyanean fountain, but brought away a few specimens of paper that had been made from the leaves of the papyrus-plant that grows there.

Since an early hour in the morning Ætna had been enveloped in thick clouds; in the evening the weather changed, and we had to walk some distance to the harbour, through pitchy darkness, and a drenching rain, which very soon wetted us through. We took shelter in the guard-house, and were treated with the greatest civility by the soldiers, and by their assistance obtained a boat, which put us on board our steamer. It rained so heavily that the phosphorescence of the sea-water was rendered visible by the agitation caused in it by each drop as it fell. At night we weighed anchor for Messina, where we arrived early on Sunday morning.

Sunday, October 17.—The beauty of Messina from the sea can scarcely be surpassed: the quay is about a mile in extent, very broad and handsome, with a curvature that adds much to its effect. In the afternoon we walked up the picturesque sandy gorge of a *fiumare* or torrent, which after heavy rain rushes down from the heights behind the town, bringing with it quantities of sand and gravel; we afterwards visited the Convent of San Gregorio. On all sides the views of the strait, the harbour, and Calabrian coast, are quite charming, with the delightful additions of cool water and luxuriant vegetation. Fine effect of heavy showers of rain about the heights of Calabria. The poor people here, as at Malta, make the prickly pear an important article of food;

a portion of the plant is generally gathered with the fruit upon it, by which means it keeps better through the winter.

Monday, October 18.—Excursion to the telegraph on the summit of the range of hills behind Messina, whence southwards was a prospect of the strait, inferior only to some we had enjoyed of the magical Bosphorus; and northwards were the Lipari Islands, and the volcano Stromboli, but obscured by haze. About a mile due south of the telegraph there is a deep and extensive hollow, which may possibly be the crater of an extinct volcano. We returned by the carriage-road called the Strada Nuova.

Tuesday, October 19.—In the morning, before leaving Messina, I took a boat and rowed out to Charybdis, which is a very strong eddy in deep water just off Messina lighthouse. In the strait there are several such eddies, particularly one off the rock Scylla, which is on the Calabrian shore, and not quite three miles and a half from the lighthouse. The morning was perfectly calm, and it did not appear to me that there would have been much danger, if accompanied by a boat, in attempting to swim in Charybdis; but the boatmen, probably to dissuade me from any lurking idea of jumping in, said that sharks were not uncommon thereabouts, and even in the harbour. When certain winds are blowing, ships refuse to answer the helm in the eddy; and in a dead calm vessels have been seen waltzing round one another for hours together. The fabulous terrors with which the ancients invested this celebrated region are not wholly without foundation. We spent the rest of the day in walking about the town, in which we noticed an unusual number of silversmiths' shops. The cathedral is remarkable for its mosaic roof, its pavement, and its altar-piece; but the whole of the interior is considerably disfigured by the bad taste exhibited in the decorations. Messina was laid waste by plague in 1743, and by the great earthquake of 1783; indeed, earthquakes are so frequent here that we were credibly informed that scarcely a month passes without the occurrence of a shock more or less violent. We left Messina in the finest weather imaginable, and from the strait enjoyed in perfection the extreme beauty of the town and heights above, and the coast of Calabria, and gazed with interest at the castle-crowned Scylla as we passed. At about two o'clock we cast anchor at Tropœa, a town in Calabria, on a rocky eminence, with woods, and vine-covered trellises, and wilder mountains in the background. We left Tropœa with Stromboli in sight, and continued our course for Naples. The evening was one of surpassing beauty; after a cloudless day we watched the sun declining immediately over the cone of Stromboli, literally

" . . . . A flaming mount, whose top
Brightness had made invisible. . . . . ."—PAR. LOST.

But after sunset the volcano reappeared, and remained in sight as long as the twilight lasted; and when it became quite dark we once or twice saw the flames. There was no wind during the night, and the sea was sufficiently smooth to reflect the young moon and the brighter stars, whilst the water curled off from the vessel's side, glowing with every variety of phosphorescence, milky, stellar, and nebulous.

> " Driven as in surges now beneath the stars,
>   With momentary stars of its own birth,
>   Fair constellated foam, still darting off
>   Into the darkness ; now a tranquil sea,
>   Outspread and bright, yet swelling to the moon."
>   COLERIDGE.

I do not understand why the phosphorescence of the Mediterranean, which we have witnessed in such perfection every night since we left the Hellespont, has not been made mention of by ancient poets; nor have I ever met with any explanation of the phenomenon that is at all satisfactory. We hauled up a bucket full of the sea-water, and dashed it about, and found that it was still luminous, and that the hand which was wetted with it was luminous also; but the effect soon went off, as if, after a certain discharge, the property or quality became exhausted. But the extreme beauty of the sight was in itself so satisfying that we felt no desire to investigate these subtle influences

> " Communicating male and female light,
>   Which two great sexes animate the world."—PAR. LOST.

Wednesday, October 20.— Passing between the Island of Capri and the main land, at half past seven in the morning we reached Naples. A thick haze hung about the bay, Vesuvius, and the mountains behind Castelamare; but a coast with a westerly aspect is rarely well seen at sunrise. After settling ourselves at the Hotel (*Crocelle*), we spent a short time at the Museo Borbonico, visited Virgil's tomb at Pausilippo, bought a few trifles at Balzani's coral shop, and in the evening went to the Theatro de' Fiorentini.

Thursday, October 21.—Museo Borbonico. Statues, bronzes, and domestic utensils of all kinds, from Herculaneum, Pompeii, and Stabiæ, with a multitude of objects of ancient art from Rome, and other parts of Italy. Bronze ornamental furniture, cooking apparatus, lamps of all forms and descriptions, earthenware and glass vessels, bread stamped with the baker's name, figs, chestnuts, olives, carubbas, cherries, wheat, barley, walnuts, I enumerate as specimens of the articles of domestic use and daily food brought to the Museum from the disinterred cities; tangible and sensible objects, which, without being intrinsically wonderful, establish an interest and a fellow-feeling between ourselves and those who nearly eighteen hundred years ago perished in a single night by the most awful catastrophe on record.

Afterwards we drove to Herculaneum, of which the portion that has been excavated underneath the houses of Portici remains in darkness, and is only to be explored by torchlight; a few of the seats of the theatre lying directly under the shaft of the well, the sinking of which originally led to the discovery of the city, are alone accessible to the light of day; however, at a very short distance, there is another excavated portion, quite open to air and daylight, where many fresco paintings, mosaic pavements, and tiles, one with the maker's name upon it, the ends of charred beams in the walls, and iron gratings in the prison-windows, still encrusted with rust and ashes, are exhibited to the curious.

Friday, October 22.—Museo Borbonico. Spent a short time amongst the bronzes, implements, and utensils, from Herculaneum and Pompeii, and then drove to Resina, in order to ascend Vesuvius. The day was one of the finest possible for the purpose. To ascend to the summit from Resina, and return, occupies about six hours. After passing the tract of vineyards, the " vicina Vesevo ora jugo," we soon arrived at the Hermitage, from whence there is a superb view of Naples and the bay, with its island break-waters, Capri, Ischia, and Procida. We then crossed a large tract of lava, stones, and scoriæ, which brought us to the foot of the cone, which we ascended in less than an hour. On reaching the top we walked, through sulphureous smoke, and over hot ashes, to the southern side of the crater, whence we obtained a most delightful view of the surrounding country and mountains beyond Pompeii and Castelamare, in the direction of Amalfi and Pæstum. Here there was a burning fissure, into which we thrust sticks, where they quickly took fire; and eggs buried in the heated soil soon became cooked. But more interesting still was the appearance of the craters, that had burst forth near the base of the mountain in an eruption of former years; for, as seen from above, not only the circular forms of these craters, but the shapes into which the accompanying ridges of lava were bent and moulded, together with the intermediate smooth fields of ashes, resembled in the closest manner the details of the irregularities seen on the surface of the moon, a similitude strongly indicating the exertion of volcanic energies in our attendant satellite; and the position of the sun, on which the shadows depended, was such as to exhibit the phenomenon to us in the greatest perfection. It happened, also, that the moon was visible in the clear sky not far from the meridian, so that, with a telescope on the summit of the mountain, we might have gazed alternately at the craters of the moon and at those of the earth.

The Phlegræan fields, on the opposite side of Naples, present a similar appearance, and whoever compares a well-executed map of the moon with a map of that volcanic district cannot fail to be struck with the resemblance, and will readily acknowledge that an Aristarchus, an Hipparchus, an Aristillus, and a Regiomontanus, may lay claim to relationship with an Astruni, a Monte Barbaro, an Avernus, and a Solfaterra; and the single insulated steep rocks or monticules, that so frequently occupy the centres of the lunar cavities, find a parallel in the small conical hill which in the year 1767 stood in the centre of a plain within the encincture of the crater of Vesuvius. Most of the lunar volcanoes, it should seem, are extinct; but observations on record render it highly probable that many are in a state of activity; nay, that their eruptions have actually been witnessed by human eyes not very long since.

Nor can any valid objection to the existence of volcanoes in the moon be founded upon the absence of an atmosphere like that of the earth; for it is not certain that the moon has *no* atmosphere, and it is not atmospheric air *alone* that supports combustion; and it must be further borne in mind that volcanic eruptions are not merely local conflagrations confined to the surface of the globe, but are the effects of convulsions caused by deep-seated internal heat, and are quite independent of an external atmosphere; and thus volcanic matter is thrown up to the surface of the ocean from depths where never plummet sounded, and bursts asunder the bars of its prison-house in yet lower depths to which the atmosphere can with difficulty be imagined to have access, and where at least it must cease to be an aeriform fluid.

The crater of Vesuvius, as we saw it, was about two miles in circumference, and perhaps 500 feet deep. The sides were precipitous all round, and at several points some fine half-detached masses hung, ready, upon the slightest tremor, to fall into the crater, in the bottom of which was a small aperture, from whence a dense column of smoke and vapour ascended continually with loud intermittent noises. A fearful passage! leading far below the base of the mountain to the chambers of the slumbering earthquake,—to lakes of perhaps *incandescent* water,—and to furnaces holding the marble and the granite rock in a state of readiness to flash into steam on the removal of the excruciating pressure to which they are subjected.

We were surprised at the great activity of the volcanic energies apparent over the whole summit of the mountain. Hundreds of acres were hot to the feet, and emitted sulphureous smoke and hot watery vapours. By digging a hole in the soil, an extemporaneous vapour bath might easily, with a little caution, have been prepared. High above us was a crag from whence a great quantity of smoke issued; indeed, in many places, the ordinary path-way lies within the crater of former eruptions. The whole of the cone is a vast barren heap of ashes, stones, scoriæ, and lava; and, owing to the immense quantity of volcanic matter extended over many square miles, the general aspect of the mountain is very desolate, excepting among the vineyards between Resina and the Hermitage. Some of the crags of the Monte di Somma, adjoining Vesuvius, are bold and precipitous.

We ascended the cone by a rough path over the hard blocks of lava, and did not experience so much fatigue as we had expected. Two ladies were of our party, and with an occasional ride in a *portandina*, and some further help from two guides, they got up very well; but their shoes were burnt and cut to pieces. We descended the cone by a path in the soft ashes, into which we sank above our ancles at every step.

Nothing can be less like the colouring of Vesuvius and the bay, at this time of the year, than the harsh body-coloured drawings sold here. Perhaps, during the heats of summer, the skies may wear that exceeding golden hue, but their tone is now quite subdued, and at sunset the distance is sobered down to a very rich and beautiful cast of grey. At night the stars are remarkably distinct.

Saturday, October 23.—Excursion to Pompeii. The drive thither occupied us about two hours, and presented little to attract attention except the beds and cliffs of modern and ancient lava, through which, in some places, the road is cut. We began at Pompeii with the Street of Tombs, and the villa of Diomed, as it is called; and then, having entered the gate of the town, we made a circuit of the whole, which occupied us about four hours. Here the usual principles of sight-seeing are reversed; and the chief interest lies, not in those objects which least, but in those which most, resemble what we are accustomed to see every day. Thus we particularly noticed the public baths, so like those at Pesth, Mehadia, and Constantinople; the fountains in private gardens, dried up indeed, but otherwise perfectly preserved, in fine mosaic and shell-work, in the most approved Pompeian show-box taste; the small chapels for the Lares and Penates, like those so often seen by the wayside dedicated to saints; and the wine and soup-shops arranged like modern *cafés*.

Not that there was any lack of nobler objects. In one part many temples stood near together, and among them the temple of Isis. This quarter of the town before the great catastrophe, with the mountain-scenery to the southward, which is finely seen from hence, must have formed a site of great beauty and elegance, though, perhaps, without any very imposing effect, for at Pompeii almost every thing is on a small scale. The greater part of the dwelling houses are quite small, and, with the exception of Diomed's villa, only one story high, and are calculated for a climate where the inhabitants live much in the open air, and when within doors wish as much as possible to exclude the heat and glare of the sun. A great variety of mosaic pavements, and fresco paintings remain. The mosaics in some instances are very fine, particularly the large one which formed the floor of a room, and represented Alexander passing the Granicus. The frescos, with few exceptions, are indifferently executed, yet the designs are of a superior description. Their effect must have been very pleasing, and, indeed, is so still, though the walls are, for the most part, roofless and bare. The tragic and comic theatres, and the amphitheatre, which is of considerable size, are very perfect. Not much sculptured stone or marble is to be seen; the use of stucco appears to have been universal. Probably not a fifth part of Pompeii has yet been excavated.

It would be vain to enter into a detail of matters bearing upon the manners and customs, physical and moral habitudes, of the ancients, as inferred from all that has been discovered at Herculaneum, Pompeii, and Stabiæ. The subject has been exhausted in well-known learned works, and it would be foreign to the present purpose to attempt any thing of the kind.

October, Sunday 24.—Quiet morning. In the afternoon to Pausilippo and Pozzuoli. After the long straight piece of road beyond the grotto of Pausilippo, we came suddenly upon a very lovely view of the sea, and the green island cliff of Nisida, and the town of Pozzuoli. The promontory of Miseno answers to Virgil's description:

> "At pius Æneas ingenti mole sepulchrum
> Imponit; suaque arma viro, remumque, tubamque,
> Monte sub aerio, qui nunc Misenus ab illo
> Dicitur, æternumque tenet per sæcula nomen."
>
> ÆNEID VI. 232.

The remains of the edifice called the Temple of Jupiter Serapis are very extensive, though it is much decayed, and has been plundered of many of its columns. It stands on a recent submarine formation, backed by an ancient volcanic cliff, now inland. The learned are not agreed upon the real character of the edifice, but three noble shafts of cipolline marble, more than forty feet high, are yet standing, the peculiarities presented by which, and by certain fragments lying near them, it is the province of the geologist, rather than of the antiquary, to explain. The surfaces of these columns are smooth and uninjured to a height of twelve feet above their pedestals, to which succeed zones of about nine feet, where the marble has been perforated by marine insects; but the remaining upper parts of the columns have undergone no such perforations, and appear to have been only subjected to the action of the weather.

From hence it is inferred that the *relative* level of land and sea has changed twice at Pozzuoli since the Christian era, and that each movement of elevation and subsidence has exceeded twenty feet: but to make this clear further facts are required, and it is especially necessary to premise that the level of the water of the Mediterranean has been ascertained to have remained unchanged for the last 2000 years. Now by the evidence of inscriptions it appears that the marble pavement of the temple was constructed about A.D. 200, manifestly not in the sea; but in 1580 a writer, named Loffredo, says that one might, in 1530, have fished from the cliff rising behind the flat land on which the temple stands; and the probability is that the subsidence took place during the eruption of the Solfaterra in 1198, and during the earthquake of 1488.

The state of things then, at the latter date, was as follows: the lower portions of the columns were embedded in pumice and other matters ejected into the sea from the Solfaterra; the middle portions were immersed in sea-water, and were subjected to its action, and to that of perforating insects; and the upper portions projected above the water, and were exposed to the action of the weather alone.

But in the year 1503 matters were again different. An Italian document, referring to the tract of land in question, says, "che va seccando el mare;" and in 1511 a Latin deed makes a grant of part of the same, and speaks of it as "desiccatum;" however, by the above statement of Loffredo, the principal elevation must have taken place after 1530. Now in 1538 the Monte Nuovo was formed: and Falconi and Toledo, eye-witnesses of the convulsion, attest to the abandonment of the shore by the sea, so that fish were taken by the inhabitants; and, amongst other things, Falconi mentions that he saw two springs in the *newly discovered ruins*. The elevation of the Temple, therefore, no doubt took place in 1538; at which time, it is worthy of remark, there was no simultaneous elevation of land, or apparent retreat of waters, at Ischia, Naples, or Castelamare. The Temple was then lost sight of until 1750, when it was rediscovered; the upper portions of the columns were then overgrown by thick bushes, and their lower portions firmly embedded in the formation of 1198, from which they were subsequently excavated. But it seems that the Temple, though at that time high and dry, was in a state of gradual subsidence; for Niccolini, the architect, who was employed on the spot in 1807, occasionally saw the pavement overflowed; but he found in 1823 that it was under water daily, and he ascertained in 1838 that the sinking had been continual, at the rate of one inch in four years; and we ourselves found the pavement under water, with a quantity of small fish swimming about, and lines of stepping-stones regularly distributed over the quadrangle.

But this is not all. In 1828 a mosaic pavement was discovered six feet below the present marble one, implying some subsidence previous to all the changes already mentioned, which had rendered it necessary to construct a new floor (the marble one) at a higher level. The date assigned to the mosaic pavement is 80 B.C., and of course it was originally constructed on dry land; hence it appears that, in the year 80 B.C., the Temple was about twelve feet above the level it occupied in 1841; that about A.D. 100 it was six feet above that level, which rate of progression probably brought it, in A.D. 400, down to its present level; that in the middle ages it was about twenty feet below its present level; and that about 1800 it was rather more than two feet above its present level; and that it is now, in 1842, slowly sinking.

It is singular that, in the course of the above investigation, both subsidence and elevation of the land should have been proved by the taking of fish. Other numerous independent proofs exist in the Bay of Baiæ of subsidences analogous to that of the Temple of Serapis. The sea, then, and not the rock, appears in such a case to be the fittest emblem of firmness and durability.*

Monday, October 25.—Museo Borbonico: engaged the whole morning amongst the bronzes of Herculaneum, and the superb collection of Etruscan vases: then to the apartment to which the epithet of *riservato*

---

* See Lyell's "Geology," Vol. II. page 384-401.

is applied; the contents of which, chiefly from Herculaneum and Pompeii, cannot be detailed on paper. One piece of sculpture, of a revolting nature, illustrated the lines in Virgil,

> "Novimus et qui te, transversa tuentibus hircis,—
> Et quo, sed faciles Nymphæ risere, sacello."—ECL. III. 8.

Among the splendid efforts of the chisel to be seen at Naples, the Hercules, perhaps, stands first. It is the finest possible embodying of a deity whose attribute is corporal strength; the figure is made up of thews and sinews, but it is light and godlike, and derives additional dignity from its attitude of repose. The Apollo with the lyre and swan is a bewitching statue; the fine flowing attitude, and the expression, are quite those of the god of music and heaven-born song. The celebrated Dirce is a wonderful piece of art, but, as a general rule, I prefer in sculpture single figures to groups. The Venus Vincitrice is colossal, with drapery from the middle; it is, indeed, a figure whose presence breathes the spirit of the opening lines of the poem of Lucretius. The Venus Callipyge, as the name denotes, is of a different character; it is said to be by Praxiteles, and though it is, in reality, an exquisite statue, I confess that, whilst I was looking at it, the tragi-comical story of the thief and servant-maid slid into my mind. In general, first-rate statues are equally beautiful from whatever side they are viewed, which is not the case with the Venus Callipyge. The Antinous presents the semblance of a very noble youth, with an open and generous expression; the statues of this vicious favourite of a vicious emperor are very numerous, and among the finest extant, and even in the firmament a constellation bears his name. Besides these, the Aristides, the head of Homer, the equestrian statues from Herculaneum, the colossal Flora, and the Agrippina, and an hundred others, deserve particular mention; but I feel that I have already lingered too long in this wonderful collection.

In the afternoon to the Palazzo Reale on the Capo di Monte. It is very large, and nearly new, and well worth visiting, were it only for the superb views of Naples, Vesuvius, and the sea, that you obtain from the windows. Called on Signor Capocci at the observatory: in the evening to the Theatre San Carlino to see the performance of Pulchinella, which, if we might judge from the roars of laughter around us, is excessively entertaining to those who are acquainted with the Neapolitan dialect.

Pulchinella is a character derived from antiquity; he appears painted on one of the Etruscan vases in the museum in a dress varying very slightly from that which he now wears on the stage; and a bronze figure was discovered at Rome in 1727 of the same personage, who turns out to be the father of fun and fancy, and the great progenitor of the illustrious family of Punch, who has contributed to the entertainment of children, of early and of larger growth, for thousands of years.

Tuesday, October 26.—Heavy rain all night—continued rain with thunder during the day. Prepa-

CAPUA.

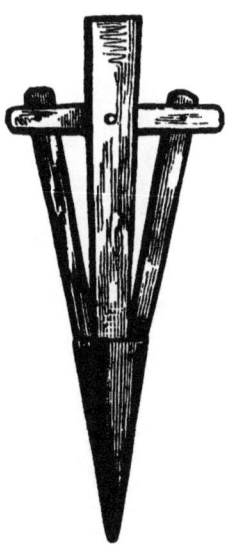

"Binæ aures, duplici aptantur dentalia dorso."
GEORG. I. 172.

rations for departure: called on Signor Capocci at the Observatory, and went over the establishment with him; the piers of the meridian instruments are of Egyptian granite, and the equatorial is mounted on blocks of lava from Vesuvius. In the evening to the Theatre of San Carlos, the most magnificent in the world.

Wednesday, October 27.—Left Naples for Rome at half-past nine in the morning in a hired carriage: the inside was occupied by ourselves, and the outside by a Sardinian Count, his servant, and the "conduttore." At one o'clock we reached Caserta, where the royal palace is ornamented with marble columns brought from the Temple of Serapis at Pozzuoli. At Capua we visited the amphitheatre of the ancient city; one of the finest ruins we have yet seen. A beautiful drawing might be made of the arched entrance, looking through it across to the opposite side of the edifice. The vast stones used in its construction are far more beautiful than brickwork, and there are many fine marble columns lying about intermixed with shrubs and verdure.

Soon afterwards an accident happened to the carriage, which occasioned some delay, and gave me an opportunity of rambling over two or three of the fields which "dives arat Capua," and of making a sketch of a plough which I saw at work. The annexed cut represents the ploughshare that was in use, and it seems to illustrate Virgil's

"Binæ aures, duplici aptantur dentalia dorso."—GEORG. I. 172.

Later in the day heavy rain came on with thunder; we crossed the River Garigliano, anciently the Liris, and at eleven o'clock at night, and not before, we reached Mola di Gaeta,* in the midst of continued thunder and lightning, with squalls of wind and torrents of rain. At Mola we stopped to sup, and, owing to circumstances unnecessary to detail, the whole party agreed that it would be better to proceed the same night, and accordingly soon after midnight we started afresh, in the midst of tremendous rain, thunder, and lightning. Among the hills near Itri five or six times successively the thunder burst upon us with distinct crashing reports like shots of artillery fired over our heads across the valley, with an impetuous torrent of rain that absolutely poured into the inside of the carriage, though all the glasses were closed. We then arrived at Fondi, where we remained about an hour, and the weather moderated a little.

Thursday, October 28.—Early in the morning our passports were examined at the frontier gates of the Papal states, near which is the narrow pass of Lautulæ, between the mountains and the sea, mentioned by Livy in the wars between the Romans and Samnites, and at eight o'clock we arrived at Terracina, and got well through the customhouse, and enjoyed our breakfast after the severe night we had passed. Terracina stands at the foot of the rocks on which

* ÆNEID VII. 1.

the ancient Anxur was built, which in Horace's time were probably whiter than at present, and less overgrown with olives, prickly pears, and shrubs. Very considerable falls in the cliff have taken place, evidently long since Horace's days, and where the fracture has occurred the newly exposed rock is of a yellowish brown. Just opposite the inn and customhouse, a very tall piece of detached rock stands apart from the main cliff; and a little further on, the ancient ruins crowning the whole are seen in an imposing situation. At about three or four miles from Terracina there was a fragment of a wall on the steep side of the mountain to our right, and on the flat marsh close to the road were trees more than sufficient to make a grove, but nothing that resembled the temple and fountain of Feronia. We then came to Bocca-fiume, which is near one of the outlets that help to drain the Pontine marshes into the sea, and to Torre-tre-Ponti, the ancient "Forum Appii," mentioned by St. Paul, and by Horace in his "Iter Brundusium." Every yard of this route is classic ground. We were now among those

> " Qui saltus, Tiberine, tuos, sacrumque Numici
> Litus arant, Rutulosque exercent vomere colles,
> Circæumque jugum, queis Jupiter Anxurus arvis
> Præsidet, et viridi gaudens Feronia luco;
> Qua Saturæ jacet atra palus, gelidusque per imas
> Quærit iter valles atque in mare conditur Ufens."
>
> ÆNEID VII. 797.

Singularly enough, soon after our encountering so

much thunder and lightning near Terracina, I accidentally met with the following passage, "In Italia, inter Terracinam et Ædem Feroniæ, turres bellicis temporibus desiere fieri, nulla non earum fulmine diruta."*

We arrived at Cisterna at about half past four in the afternoon, having nearly passed the Pontine marshes, which looked unusually wretched and dreary owing to the late rains, and were neither sea nor good dry land. Here we remained for the night; the rooms struck damp and chilly, so we lighted a fire, and spread open our luggage which had been exposed to the night's rain, and smoked cigars vigorously until we retired. We were disturbed at two o'clock in the morning by thunder and lightning, with dreadful squalls of wind.

Friday, October 29.—We started at half past six in the morning in a fresh thunder-storm, with vivid lightning and heavy rain. On the road observed a great many olive-trees, some in small plantations, and others growing in wild places amongst fern and heather. Their foliage has a pleasing silvery tint, not unlike that of green tea. The vines were in many places trained gracefully on light trellis-work, made with the marsh reeds.

Continued rain with thunder all the way by Velletri, Genzano, and Aricia, to Albano, which we reached at about half past eleven o'clock; here we breakfasted, and remained nearly three hours, and then continued our journey, in the same weather,

* PLIN. II. 56.

to Rome, where we arrived at about five o'clock, and fixed ourselves in the Piazza del Popolo at Melloni's Hotel (*Isles Britanniques*). In the evening it cleared up, and the moon shone brightly; between eight and nine o'clock I took a quiet stroll round the fine Egyptian obelisk and fountain close at hand, and up the Via del Corso. All was hushed and still to a degree I had never before witnessed at so early an hour in a great capital; the shops were closed, only a few people were to be seen, and I heard little more than my own footsteps and the plashing of the numerous fountains.

Saturday, October 30.—At Rome: weather still wet, with thunder and lightning. In the morning to the Vatican. Here we saw Raphael's four celebrated frescos of Constantine, Heliodorus, the school of Athens, and the fire in Borgo San Spirito, painted on the walls of four different rooms or halls, which are named after them, which also contain many other frescos, all designed by Raphael himself, though some were coloured by his pupils. The ceiling in the hall of Constantine, representing the idol Mercury falling in pieces before the presence of the symbol of the crucifix set up in opposition to it, struck me as not being in the best taste. Here also were some superb pictures, amongst which Raphael's Transfiguration hung supreme; and here, agreeably to the rule laid down with so much humour in the "Vicar of Wakefield," we did not fail to "praise the works of Pietro Perugino."

Thence to St. Peter's, with which the noble piazza, the colonnade, the Egyptian obelisk, and the two superb fountains, unite to form perhaps the most astonishing assemblage in Europe. But neither the exterior, nor even does the interior of St. Peter's, before you come to measure and compare, strike you as being wonderfully vast, so exquisite are the proportions, and so wholly in character with all around you are objects of a large size. This is particularly observable in the colossal equestrian statues of Charlemagne and Constantine in the vestibule or covered portico that leads along the whole front. With respect to the structure itself:—

> "Enter: its grandeur overwhelms thee not;
> And why? it is not lessened; but thy mind,
> Expanded by the genius of the spot,
> Has grown colossal."—BYRON.

I must, however, confess that, agreeably to a first impression, there was something about the roof of the nave not altogether suited to the character of a sacred edifice, and that parts of the building may be said to have an appearance of coldness, notwithstanding the extreme richness and profuse variety of the marbles, and the extraordinary copies of the most celebrated pictures in mosaic; but on arriving underneath the cupola,

> — "The vast and wondrous Dome,
> To which Diana's marvel was a cell,"

covered to the very summit with gigantic designs also in mosaic, the "musical immensity" and colouring of which removes all idea of overwhelming size—every tendency to criticism gives way to wonder and admiration, not only whilst you are within the edifice, but afterwards, when the mind reflects leisurely on all that has been presented to it, and is at liberty coolly to admit the statistics, and peruse the measurements of a building that triumphs over all our ordinary notions of dimension. The celebrated bronze baldacchino, or dais, by Bernini, underneath the dome, is about 120 feet high, which may serve to convey some idea of the space that is required to render an ornament on such a scale admissible.

After taking a cup of excellent chocolate, we drove to some of the shops for cameos, pastes, and trifles of that description, and then to the Coliseum, or Flavian amphitheatre. We found it in a more ruinous condition than we had expected; like all the edifices of ancient Rome, it has suffered severely from time, war, earthquakes, civil dissension, and abuse of the materials; and its effect is marred by the modern buttresses and arches that have been erected in order to support some of its parts, and by the ugly wooden painted shrines set up round the arena; but the mechanical support of the one, and the consecrating influence of the other, are essential to its preservation from further rapid decay and continued pillage: in fact, the Farnese palace, and other buildings, were constructed with materials actually quarried out of the Coliseum. Its elliptical shape is very fine, and greatly relieves the massiveness of the whole. From some points of view, owing to its vast size, and the grass and shrubs that have overgrown it, rock and foliage as it were intermixed, the idea of its being a ruined edifice begins to fade away, and you are half persuaded that you are contemplating some object of natural scenery, until the reality is brought back by an inspection of the arena, and the recollection of the atrocious festivals celebrated there for the delight of an emperor and of fifty thousand of his subjects at once. Nor does it appear that the Coliseum is immaculate in other respects. A living author says, " When I wandered over this scene of guilt, I could not but regard it as a monument of prodigal folly and savage sensuality. Moreover, from the haste with which it was run up, there are numerous architectural eyesores, which, with its cumbrous attic, render it very inferior to the elegant amphitheatre at Pola, in Istria."* This amphitheatre we should in all probability have seen had we returned by way of Trieste. Notwithstanding the accounts of ancient writers who attest the fact, and the evidence afforded by the holes visible in the upper cornice of the outer wall, in which the poles were fixed, it is not easy to understand how a canopy or awning could have been extended over the whole. The Coliseum was commenced by Vespasian, and finished by Titus, who prolonged the festivals of its dedication to an hundred days, and is reported to have wept bitterly at their conclusion; an exhibition of feeling that resulted, no doubt,

* Smyth on " Roman medals," page 63.

from the reaction naturally succeeding intense and protracted excitement, and the consciousness of misspent time and treasure.

Parties are frequently made to visit the Coliseum by moonlight; but whilst marshalling your thoughts in a train suited to the scene — calling up the dead within the magic circle of the arena — or crowding the ruin with Cellini's demon audience, the illusion is apt to be wholly put to flight by finding that you have stepped up to the ankles in water, and by noisy visitors, and the annoyance of the key-bugle echoing through the corridors. An ancient ruin, to produce its full effect, should stand in a solitary place, and be seen in bright and tranquil sunshine, with all its details and adjuncts, even down to insects, reptiles, and wild flowers.

After the vivacity and stir of Naples the solemn stillness pervading Rome is very remarkable, and quite in keeping with the spectacle of its ancient monuments in decay; and in almost every part of the city you are refreshed by the sight and sound of the waters of the numerous fountains.

Sunday, October 31. — Divine service at the English chapel. Thunder and rain. In the afternoon to the

". . . . . . —Pantheon,—pride of Rome!"

" Relic of nobler days, and noblest arts !
  Despoiled, yet perfect, with thy circle spreads
  A holiness appealing to all hearts—
  To art a model; and to him who treads
  Rome for the sake of ages, glory sheds

>   Her light through thy sole aperture; to those
>   Who worship, here are altars for their beads,
>   And they who feel for genius may repose
>   Their eyes on honoured forms, whose busts around them close."
>   BYRON.

Thence to the church of Santa Maria sopra Minerva, to see Michael Angelo's statue of our Saviour, and to the church of San Pietro in Vincoli, to see his well-known statue of Moses. Thence to the Batisterio of Constantine, and the Church of San Giovanni in Laterano, in which is the famous Corsini chapel, and where also the cloisters are well worthy of a visit. Thence to the Scala Santa, or Holy Staircase, said to be that which led up to Pilate's Judgment-Hall; we saw many devout penitents, men, women, and children, ascending it upon their knees. To the Corso, and Pincian Hill, whence we saw the sun set behind St. Peter's.

Monday, November 1.—Festival of All Saints. Divine service in the Sistine chapel, where the pope and cardinals were all assembled. The singing was not particularly fine. We looked with great interest at Michael Angelo's sublime frescoes on the ceiling and walls of the chapel, but they require a very bright day. We then paid a second visit to St. Peter's, after which we returned to the Sistine chapel, but we soon came away, as the ceremony was very tedious. Visited some of our acquaintance whom we met here. Evening cold and wet, and we felt glad of a fire.

Tuesday, November 2.—The Vatican. Saw a considerable portion of the wonders of this never-ending collection. The Antinous, the Laocoon, and the Apollo, are in themselves a gallery. The Antinous is a representation of manly beauty not to be surpassed. The right arm is wanting, and the readiness with which the mind supplies such a defect is a singular proof of the abstract quality of sculpture of a high order. We found the Laocoon, as we had expected, a master-piece of art, but the art itself is, perhaps, too apparent. Laocoon's two children assist in telling the story, and their attitudes are managed, and their proportions subdued, so as to remove all formality from the outline of the group: they were probably never intended for objects of minute attention, but were introduced to relieve and sustain the eye in subservience to the principal figure. Pliny makes mention of the Laocoon as the joint work of three Rhodian artists, Agesander, Polydorus, and Athenodorus. An extant inscription speaks of Athenodorus, son of Agesander; and upon this the pleasing conjecture has been founded, that Polydorus also was his son, enabling us to picture to ourselves the father and his two sons at work upon the same group, and suggesting the possibility of the three figures being portraits of the sculptors themselves, accounting at the same time, in some degree, for the evident disagreement of the stature of the children with their apparent ages.

The Apollo Belvedere, or Apollo Venator, is probably the finest statue in the world. After dwelling a while in undivided attention on the godlike image, we mused with feelings akin to awe upon the operations of the mind of the sculptor that could body forth such an expression, and the hand that could turn the marble to such a shape, positively floating with grace and beauty.

> " Or view the Lord of the unerring bow,
> The God of life, and poesy, and light—
> The Sun in human limbs arrayed, and brow
> All radiant from his triumph in the fight;
> The shaft hath just been shot—the arrow bright
> With an immortal's vengeance; in his eye
> And nostril, beautiful disdain, and might,
> And majesty, flash their full lightnings by,
> Developing in that one glance the Deity."
>
> BYRON.

The fervours of this glowing description may be mitigated by contrasting it with that of Master Edmund Warcupp, who wrote and "translated out of the originals for general satisfaction," in 1660. Among other statues " of the politest marble," he says, "in the fifth armory (of the Vatican) is the Apollo Pitheo, with a serpent at his feet, and carcase having a piece of cloth upon one arm, a bow and arrows in his hand, and all over naked."

The Apollo is nearly seven feet high, exclusive of the plinth. From certain technical indications in the folds of the mantle, and from the manner in which the marble is joined, as well as from its quality and condition, and from the support given to the left foot, and to the right arm, it is finally argued that this statue was never designed to be an object of public worship, that it has never suffered exposure to the outward air, and that it was in all probability copied from a bronze, expressly for some rich Roman virtuoso, to adorn the gallery of his villa.

We also paid our *devoirs* to the statue of the Venus, seated on a shell. It is smaller than life, and extremely lovely. Thence to the Museum of the Capitol, and saw the Faun in rosso-antico, the Hercules in gilt bronze, the Cupid and Psyche, the Capitoline Venus, and the sublime and touching statue called the Dying Gladiator. But gladiatorial combats were not in vogue in the best ages of sculpture, to which this production must be assigned; and the cord round the neck, and the accompaniments of the sword and shield, and the horn, seem rather to confer upon the dying man the title of herald, or attendant upon some warlike chieftain, in a capacity, perhaps, similar to that of Misenus,—

> " Misenum Æoliden, quo non præstantior alter
> Ære ciere viros, Martemque accendere cantu.
> Hectoris hic magni fuerat comes; Hectora circum
> Et lituo pugnas insignis obibat, et hasta."
>
> ÆNEID VI. 164.

This statue is very probably a copy of the bronze mentioned by Pliny (Lib. xxxiv. 8.) as the masterpiece of Ctesilaus. The same author, however, when on the subject of bronzes, says of another statuary, that he was " marmore felicior, ideoque clarior."

Quitting the Museum, and passing by the superb gilt bronze equestrian statue of Marcus Aurelius, we visited the Tarpeian rock. "Is this, ye gods, the Capitolian hill?" and yet any one falling into the dirty court-yard beneath would infallibly meet with a broken neck. But it is evident, from the excavations that have been made, that the level of the soil was originally many feet below what it is at present, and knowing that in Livy's time the rock had crumbled away from the top, we now see enough to shew that the precipice may once have been of very considerable height. We continued our walk by the beautiful remains of the Temple of Jupiter Tonans, the Temple of Fortune, and the arch of Septimius Severus, along part of the Via Sacra, with the Farnese gardens on the right, and the Basilica of Constantine on the left, to the Arch of Titus, and so, by the once "lautæ Carinæ," to the Coliseum, and the Arch of Constantine. No volume of any moderate size could give a detailed account of the remains of this portion of ancient Rome. With regard to these scenes, consecrated in part to time-honoured fictions, which Niebuhr and others bid us throw to oblivion, I cannot refrain from quoting one of Wordsworth's later sonnets:—

> "These old credulities to nature dear,
>   Shall they no longer bloom upon the stock
>   Of History, stript naked as a rock
>   'Mid a dry desert? What is it we hear?
>   The glory of infant Rome must disappear,
>   Her morning splendours vanish, and their place
>   Know them no more. If Truth, who veiled her face
>   With those bright beams, yet hid it not, must steer
>   Henceforth a humbler course, perplexed and slow,
>   One solace yet remains for us who came
>   Into this world in days when story lacked
>   Severe research, that in our hearts we know
>   How, for exciting youth's heroic flame,
>   Assent is power, belief the soul of fact."

But here also in a multitude of instances Truth

puts on her most serious garb. Witness only the basso-relievos upon the Arch of Titus, representing the spoils brought from the Temple of Jerusalem; or those upon the Arch of Septimius Severus, where the erasement of the name of Geta and the defacement of his image—evidences of violence and of the hatred that conceived and brought forth fratricide—survive to this day on the monument erected to the honour of the father;—who can contemplate these, and not depart sadder and wiser from the presence of relics, and the study of lessons, such as no other locality can furnish?

In the afternoon to the Vigna Palatina, a villa belonging to Mr. Mills. The view from the garden is singularly interesting and beautiful. When you face the Aventine Hill, you look down upon what was the Circus Maximus; on the left, in the distance, are the heights of Albano, with the country between, and richly coloured masses of ruins in the foreground; and on the right, a great part of Rome, with St. Peter's. The garden is bounded by the ruined walls of the palace of Augustus, and the house itself stands immediately over some of the imperial apartments, now below the level of the soil. These are best seen about noon on a bright day. Thence to Thorvaldsen's studio, where we admired the statue of a youth playing on a pipe, and some pretty basso-relievos.

Wednesday, November 3.—The first fine day since we left Naples. Rome is certainly damp and chilly at this time of the year: a fire becomes desirable every evening. The sun shone brilliantly all day, but a little more warmth would have been agreeable.

Again to Saint Peter's. We ascended to the summit of the cupola, and obtained a near view of the gigantic mosaics, which at a distance produce an uniform brilliancy and lightness of effect, perhaps unattainable by paintings. Some of the pieces of which they are composed are two inches square. The pen, represented in the hand of one of the evangelists, is seven feet in length, which may give some idea of the scale upon which these mosaics are executed. The architectural history of St. Peter's is very interesting. An hemispherical dome, surmounted by a heavy weight, has, on mechanical principles, a tendency to burst at the sides, in consequence of which property, before the completion of the dome in 1590, it was judged necessary to gird it round with enormously massive bands of iron, and others have since been added. They are visible at intervals partially embedded in masonry. Sir Christopher Wren, in building St. Paul's cathedral, took the precaution to erect the lantern, ball, and cross, on the summit of a pyramid of brick-work, round which the frame-work of the dome was afterwards constructed in carpentry of comparative lightness, forming a whole of amazing stability.

A degree of imperfection of another kind in St. Peter's arises from the rejection of Peruzzi's plan of a Greek cross, of which the four arms are equal, and the final adoption of the Latin cross, as originally designed by Bramante; for from the form of the Latin cross is derived the great length of the nave, which mars the effect of the dome, both within and without, by throwing it in both instances too far back from those portions of the building which must first catch the eye; nor has the front of the portico by Carlo Maderno escaped criticism; nevertheless, the whole structure stands confessedly a matchless wonder, nor would it be easy to say by how many definable degrees of magnificence St. Peter's excels every other existing edifice.

Again to the Antinous, the Laocoon, and the Apollo, and thence to the Etruscan cabinet in the Vatican. Here are a multitude of beautiful vases, and other antiquities; but this collection is poor after that of Naples. On one of the Etruscan vases was a representation of cock-fighting, and on another a caricature of Jupiter and Mercury, not unlike our modern clown and pantaloon; Jupiter with a grotesque head thrust through the rounds of a ladder, about to scale a lady's window, and Mercury performing a sort of farcical Leporello-like character, with a lamp in his hand.

Again to Thorvaldsen's studio, and Mr. Mills' villa. The day was remarkably fine, and every part of the view was seen to perfection. In a corner of the garden an acanthus was growing by the side of a broken Corinthian capital, on which the sculptured leaves really seemed to be a copy of those of the living plant.

Thursday, November 4.—High mass performed in church near the Piazza del Popolo. The pope attended in person, and we saw him arrive in state, and assist at the ceremony, which, however, was very tedious. In the afternoon to the superb new church of St. Paul, outside the walls of Rome, and took the following antiquities in the course of our drive;—the Ponte Rotto, the ancient Pons Sublicius, the Temple of Fortuna Virilis, the Temple of Vesta, the Temple of Pudicitia Patriciana, the Arch of Septimius Severus in Foro Boario, the Arch of Janus Quadrifrons, the Cloaca Maxima, the Mons Testaceus, the Tomb of Caius Cestius, and the Theatre of Marcellus.

The Column of Trajan, and the Column of Marcus Aurelius, both adorned with continued spirals of basso-relievos, are, perhaps, the most remarkable monuments of the kind in Rome. The Column of Trajan stands on a spot once the centre of a Forum, renowned for its magnificence, but which lay for a length of time buried under an accumulation of earth and rubbish; however, extensive excavations have been effected, laying open the column to its base, together with perhaps one-half of the area of the Forum. The basso-relievos relate to Trajan's two Dacian campaigns, and contain authentic representations of the arms, implements, vestments, ceremonies, and tactics of the age, peculiarly interesting after a voyage down the Danube. On the column of Marcus Aurelius are, in like manner, exhibited the wars of that emperor with the Quadi and Marcomanni. The great number of ancient obelisks of Egyptian granite erected in the various Piazzas is another remarkable feature in Rome.

Friday, November 5.—Picture gallery at the Palazzo de' Conservatori. Noticed particularly two Sybils, one by Guercino, and the other by Domenichino, and the St. Sebastian, also by Domenichino. Rode in the afternoon about the Campagna. Saw several persons shooting larks, of which great quantities are thus killed. A running brook accompanied the great aqueduct that stretches across the Campagna towards the city; no doubt the same stream which used to be conveyed in the channel over the arches.

Saturday, November 6.—Preparations for departure. Rode in the afternoon to Frescati; lovely view of the expanse of the Campagna bounded by the Appennines, whose extreme visible fluctuation is Mount Soracte, with Rome and the sea in the distance, a little towards the left. Noticed several different kinds of ploughs at work. Weather quite lovely.

Sunday, November 7.—Quiet morning. In the afternoon to the gardens on the Pincian hill. Public lottery and music. Sky brilliantly clear, but the air chilly.

Monday, November 8.—Left Rome for Civita Vecchia at four in the morning by a diligence, and arrived there at noon. The Castor steamer, however, which had been advertised at Rome for to-day, was not in the harbour.

Tuesday, November 9.—At Civita Vecchia. Steamer not arrived. Weather lovely and calm. We amused ourselves as well as we could by walking about and gathering shells on the sea-shore, and I made the accompanying sketch of a plough in the neighbouring fields, in using which the ploughman frequently stands upon the "binæ aures" behind the "stiva," or plough-handle, and so *rides* along the furrow, giving additional force to Virgil's metaphor of "imos currus."

Wednesday, November 10.—Early in the morning the steamer appeared in sight. We got on board in due time, and at about eleven o'clock we bade adieu to fair Italy, and got under way for Marseilles. On board we found Reschid Pacha and suite, on his route to Paris, and some Moorish passengers going to Leghorn, and some English officers from India by way of Alexandria and Malta, who apprised us of poor Monro's death at the latter place, the intelligence of which had not yet reached us. We made Cape Argentaro at about half-past three o'clock, and saw the sun set nearly over the island of Elba.

Thursday, November 11.—At about five o'clock in the morning we came to an anchor off Leghorn, and after setting some of our passengers on shore, and taking on board others, we got under way at about eleven o'clock, with a fresh wind, and a somewhat threatening sky, and a great deal of swell, but happily at night it fell calm.

Friday, November 12.—Bright sunshine and calm sea. About eight in the morning we discovered the Maritime Alps covered with snow, and at noon passed close by the Stæchades Islands. At about two o'clock we were off Hyères, and saw on our left the Médes rocks. The sun still shone brilliantly, but the

CIVITA VECCHIA, near Rome.

"Huic à stirpe pedes temo protentus in octo,
Binæ aures, duplici aptantur dentalia dorso.
Cæditur et tilia antè jugo levis, altaque fagus,
Stivaque, quæ currus à tergo torqueat imos."—GEORG. I. 171.

wind was very cold, and stronger than was agreeable; but it again fell calm at sunset, and at about ten o'clock at night we arrived at Marseilles, and took up our quarters at the Hotel (*d'Orient*).

Saturday, November 13.—Cleared our baggage at the customhouse, and walked about the town, which is very handsome and clean. Excessively cold wind, with clouds of dust. To the theatre in the evening.

Sunday, November 14.—Walked about the town, and up to the Telegraph station, commanding a superb view of Marseilles and the sea. Weather warmer than yesterday: blue sky and bright sun.

Monday, November 15.—Left Marseilles for Lyons at five o'clock in the morning. The scenery of the Rhone is extremely pretty; but for hours together we passed through whole tracts of vineyard and corn-land quite laid waste by the violence and extent of the recent inundations. All the hills of any elevation were capped with snow. Bright sunshine and cold wind.

Tuesday, November 16.—After travelling all night, we arrived at Lyons at seven in the evening.

Wednesday, November 17.—At Lyons. Weather cold and damp to the greatest degree. The whole town enveloped in thick fog. Here the junction of the Rhone and Saone takes place, and during the late inundations the water rose to a most alarming height in the lower stories of the houses on the quays.

Visited the Museum, which contains some remarkably good modern pictures by Lyonnese artists, and some very fine small antique bronzes, and other cabinet curiosities. There was also a very perfect mosaic pavement on a large scale, representing a circus and Roman chariot-race. The "carceres," or starting places, are clearly depicted; a slave appears standing ready to dash water over the glowing wheels as the chariots come in, and the positions of the three pillars or "metæ," at each extremity of the oblong inclosure, or "spina," in the middle of the circus, round which the chariots were driven several times, shew that two very sharp turnings must be made in each circuit, affording on the whole a lively commentary upon Horace's

" . . . . . Metaque fervidis
Evitata rotis . . . . . . "

Two chariots were represented overthrown, out of, I think, six, in contention for the prize. Two officials stood in the centre of the "spina," one holding a palm-branch, and the other a garland. The "metæ" were always kept on the left hand of the charioteers.

We left Lyons at nine o'clock in the evening.

Thursday, November 18.—At one o'clock we arrived at Chalons sur Saone. Weather wet and cold, and the general wintry appearance of the country we passed through struck us forcibly after the warm regions we had so lately quitted. At Chalons we met with one of our acquaintance, who left Malta on the 28th of September, and had been to London, and had arrived thus far on his return to Alexandria. We left Chalons in the evening, and travelled all night.

Friday, November 19.—Autun, Saulieu, Avalon, Vermanton, and Auxerre.

Saturday, November 20. — Arrived at Paris. Found letters at the Post-office, containing painful intelligence, which damped the pleasure of the remainder of our journey.

Sunday, November 21.— At Paris. Quiet day.

Monday, November 22.— At Paris. Walked and drove about, and visited some of our acquaintance.

Tuesday, November 23. — Some years having elapsed since our last visit to Paris, the Luxor obelisk, the fountains, and the general embellishments of the Place Louis Quinze, were quite new to us. Weather wet, with a gale of wind.

Wednesday, November 24.— A bright sunny day. Had two portraits taken by the process of the Daguerrotype. After several complete failures, the portraits were produced, but so unsatisfactory were they, that for one of them we paid half the money rather than take it away, and the other we threw into the fire soon after we got home. All the portraits that I have ever seen taken by this process are not only unpleasing, but unlike the originals; and it is perhaps not difficult to account for this. Although the bare outline must be correct, yet the prepared metallic plate has a disagreeable glare, and, owing to the chemical properties of light, is variously affected by images which are necessarily of various hues depending upon the complexions of the sitters; for which reason there are generally some features and lines unduly exaggerated, and others smoothed down, so as to convey the truth, but not the whole truth; and I once saw a Daguerrotype portrait taken of a person with a ruddy complexion and clear bald head, which came out wholly falsified, by representing, not the features of the original, but those of a swarthy individual dressed in hair powder. Moreover, our idea of any person is not formed from the expression of the countenance at any given moment, but is a general average of all the impressions made upon us by it at different times, an effect which a portrait painted in several sittings, which occupy time, may well express, but which the momentary process of the Daguerrotype may hardly succeed in producing.

The French seem to exult over the destruction of the Waterloo trophies by the late fire at the Tower of London.

Thursday, November 25.—Left Paris at nine o'clock in the morning.

Friday, November 26.—Arrived at Calais late in the afternoon.

Saturday, November 27.—Crossed to Dover, where we remained a few hours, and in the afternoon started for London, where, late at night, we arrived, with thankful hearts, in perfect health and safety.

APPENDIX.

APPENDIX.

The books in the annexed alphabetical list will be found, in connexion with the classics in general, both useful and interesting as works of reference before or after a tour such as this Journal comprises. Some few of them would probably be selected as travelling companions. Though the tour happens not to include Greece, yet, as such a route would in most cases lead the tourist thither, certain works relating to that country have been inserted.

The numbers prefixed within brackets are those of Mr. James Bohn's Catalogue. *London*, 1840.

1 [250] Antichità di Ercolano. 9 vols. fol. *Napoli*, 1755-92.

2 Bartoli's Plates of the Basso-relievos of Trajan's Column. *Roma, s. a.*

3 Bartoli's Plates of the Basso-relievos of the Column of Marcus Aurelius. *Roma.*

4 Bulwer's Last Days of Pompeii. 8vo. *London*, 1840.

5 [1768] Choiseul-Gouffier, Voyage Pittoresque de la Grèce. 2 vols. in 3, fol. *Paris*, 1782-1822.

6 [2129] Cramer's Ancient Italy. 2 vols. 8vo. 1826.

7 [2131] Cramer's Ancient Greece. 3 vols. 8vo. 1828.

8 [2461] Dibdin's Tour in France and Germany. 3 vols. 8vo. 1821.

9 [2573] Dodwell's Thirty Views in Greece. Folio. *London,* 1819.

10 [3175] Gell and Gandy's Pompeiana. 8vo. *London,* 1817–19.

11 [3176] Gell's Pompeiana. 2 vols. 8vo. *Lond.* 1827.

12 [3440] Hamilton's Campi Phlegræi. 3 vols. in 1, Folio. *Naples,* 1776–79.

13 [4036] Italia, Sicilia, &c. 5 vols. 8vo. *Torino,* 1838.

14 Marsigli, Description du Danube, &c. 6 vols. fol. *La Haye,* 1744.

15 Matthews' Diary of an Invalid. 2 vols. 8vo. 1822.

16 Melling, Voyage Pittoresque de Constantinople. Folio. *Paris,* 1809–19.

17 [5138] Lady Mary Wortley Montague's Letters. 3 vols. 12mo. 1763.

18 [5150] Montfauçon, L'Antiquité Expliquée, &c. 15 vols. fol. *Paris,* 1724.

19 Murray's Guide to Southern Germany. 8vo. *London,* 1840.

20 Murray's Hand-Book for Travellers in the East. 8vo. *London,* 1840.

21 Murray's Guide to Northern Germany. 8vo. *London,* 1841.

22 [5254] Musée Français. 6 vols. fol. *Paris,* 1803–22.

23 [5259] Museo Borbonico. 12 vols. 4to. *Nap.* 1824.

24 [2578] D'Ohsson, Tableau Général de l'Empire Othoman. 3 vols. fol. 1787–1821.

25 [5614] Pausanias, Description of Greece (Translated from the Greek). 3 vols. 8vo. *Lond.* 1824.

26 [5814] Piranesi, Veduta di Roma. 2 vols. fol. *Roma, s. a.*

27 Pompeii. (From the Library of Entertaining Knowledge.) 2 vols. 8vo. 1836.

28 Rossini, Antichità Romane. Fol. *Roma,* 1822-23.

29 [6443] Rossini, Antichità di Pompeii. Fol. 1837.

30 Saint Non, Voyage Pittoresque de Naples et de Sicile. 5 vols. fol. *Paris,* 1781–86.

31 Smith, Dictionary of Greek and Roman Antiquities. 8vo. *London,* 1842.

32 [6960] Smyth on Roman Medals. 4to. *Bedford,* 1834.

33 Smyth's Sicily. 4to. *London,* 1824.

34 Starke's Continental Travellers' Guide. 8vo. 1824.

35 [8177] Wordsworth's Athens and Attica. 8vo. *London,* 1837.

36 Zahn, Ornements de Pompei, d'Herculanum, et de Stabiæ. Royal folio. *Berlin,* 1828.

NOTES.

Note to page 13.

In a private letter which I wrote from Ratisbon to a friend in England, I find an account of two other instruments of torture omitted in the Journal. One of these was a chair with sharp wooden spikes, upon which prisoners were condemned to sit with stone weights placed in their laps.

This machine seems analogous to the κνάφος mentioned by Herodotus. "Κνάφος, suivant l'explication de Suidas, d'Hésychius, et de Timée, est un instrument armé de pointes, assez ressemblant aux chardons dont se servent les foulons, sur lesquels on faisoit mourir les criminels." — Note 256 to Larcher's *Translation of Herodotus.* CLIO, XCII.

It also calls to mind the "harrows of iron" under which David put the inhabitants of Rabbah. — 2 Sam. xii. 31; 1 Chron. xx. 3.

The other was a kind of ladder furnished in the place of steps with sharply edged triangular prisms of hard wood, revolving on pivots, over which the criminal was repeatedly drawn by ropes, and suffered to fall back rapidly by his own weight. When we saw it, it stood against the wall at an angle of about forty-five degrees. It was probably very similar to the κλίμαξ, or ladder, made mention of by Aristophanes among other instruments of torture.

ΑΙΑΚΟΣ.

καὶ πῶς βασανίζω;

ΞΑΝΘΙΑΣ.

πάντα τρόπον, ἐν κλίμακι
δήσας, κρεμάσας, ὑστριχίδι μαστιγῶν, δέρων,
στρεβλῶν, ἔτι δ' ἐς τάς ῥῖνας ὄξος ἐγχέων,
πλίνθους ἐπιτιθείς, πάντα τἄλλα.—*Ranæ*, 633.

Note to page 14.

VALHALLA. (Scandin. *i.e.* the hall of those who died by violence), in the mythology of the ancient Saxons, Scandinavians, Swedes, &c., the Paradise of Odin, where, after death, the souls of warriors were believed to be feasted by Odin.—*London Encyclopædia*, 1839.

Also see Smith's " Dictionary of Greek and Roman Antiquities." *London*, 1842. *Article* CEREVISIA.

See also the Notes to Herbert's " Helga."

Note to page 46.

The Atmeidan, or Hippodrome, is little more than the site of the ancient Roman Circus commenced on that spot by Septimius Severus. The Obelisks and Brazen Column are all that remain of the decorations of the *Spina* of the Circus.

Note to page 66.

It may be observed, with respect to the ceremonies of both the Dervishes of Constantinople and Scutari, that dances of various kinds have been from the most ancient times closely connected with religion. It is quite needless to adduce learned authorities on a point so well known: even David, in dancing before the ark, was in all probability not yielding to a sudden impulse of ecstatic worship, but carrying out, in the purest and most reverential spirit, the observance of an ancient oriental custom, although established amongst idolatrous nations. One of my acquaintance, a young lady, lately arrived from the East Indies, shewed me not long since a drawing she had made of a Hindoo girl dancing before an idol. But the movements of the howling Dervishes, if not grossly corrupted, are surely derived from an impure source. Their rites are exactly described by the expression, "μέλος τι κνισμῷ αὐλούμενον."—*Athen.* lib. 14.

Note to page 85.

"Many have imagined the Carubba to have been the favourite diet of the Lotophagi, and perhaps it was so; but its occasional use in the present day can bear no comparison to the claims of the rhamnus lotus, a shrub I have met with in such abundance in Africa as to indicate it likely to have been the general food of a primitive people."—Smyth's *Sicily.*

Note to page 89.

I forgot in the Journal to mention the very ancient, but small and delicate race of dogs, which, it is said, you may still meet with at Malta; but during our stay we never saw one of them, nor even was there one, whether of the true breed or not, exhibited to us, or offered to us for sale; which would surely not have been the case, particularly as there was a lady of our party, if any of the little animals had been forthcoming. One of our fellow-travellers, who knew Malta well, assured me that he had seen specimens of the breed, but that they would scarcely bear removal from their native climate. The following passage is from the chapter *De la sotte vanité*, in La Bruyère's Translation of the Greek of Theophrastus; among the characteristics of the vain man he instances the following, "S'il lui meurt un petit chien, il l'enterre, lui dresse une épitaphe avec ces mots: *Il étoit de race de Malte.*" Καὶ κυναρίου δὲ τελευτήσαντος, αὐτῷ μνῆμα ποιῆσαι, καὶ στηλίδιον ποιήσας ἐπιγράψαι, ΚΛΑΔΟΣ ΜΕΛΙΤΑΙΟΣ.

ΠΕΡΙ ΜΙΚΡΟΦΙΛΟΤΙΜΙΑΣ.

Note to page 122.

"The Coliseum is of an elliptical form, and covers nearly six acres of ground. The major axis is 616 feet, and the minor 510, with a height of 160."—SMYTH *on Roman Medals.*

Tacitus says (*Annal.* xiv. 20), "Erant qui Cn. Pompeium incusatum à senioribus ferrent, quòd mansuram theatri sedem posuisset: nam anteà subitariis gradibus, et scenâ in tempus structâ, ludos edi solitos: vel si vetustiora repetas, stantem populum spectavisse; ne, si consideret, theatro dies totos ignaviâ continuaret." And thus the ancient Romans *lapped* at the stream of pleasure, not *bowing down* upon their knees to drink; and so went forth to conquest. In how altered and debased a spirit were the spectators of after-times assembled in the Coliseum!

The gorgeous theatrical canopies of the Romans must have produced a remarkable effect, independent of their practical utility, transmitting variously coloured light over a multitude whose numbers were computed by tens of thousands, and upon an arena that was itself upon occasion strewn with a brilliantly tinted mixture of borax and cinnabar. In them the Emperor Caligula found materials for practical jesting, when, "gladiatorio munere, reductis interdum flagrantissimo sole velis, emitti quenquam vetabat."— *Suetonius*. Upon them the wit of Martial has been exercised, and they have furnished Lucretius with imagery illustrative of some of the most exalted topics to be found in his poems. Speaking of colours, he says,

" Nam certè jacere ac perciri multa videmus,
 Non solùm ex alto, penitùsque, ut diximus antè,
 Verùm de summis ipsum quoque sæpè colorem:
 Et volgò faciunt id lutea, russaque vela,
 Et ferrugina, quòm magnis intenta theatris
 Per malos volgata trabesque, trementia flutant.
 Namque ibi consessum caveaï subter, et omnem
 Scenaï speciem, patrum, matrumque, deorumque,

> Inficiunt, coguntque suo fluitare colore:
> Et quanto circum magè sunt inclusa theatri
> Mœnia, tam magis hæc intus, perfusa lepore,
> Omnia conrident, conreptâ luce diei."
>
> *Lucretius*, IV. 70-81.

And again, speaking of storms,

> " Dant etiam sonitum patuli super æquora mundi,
> Carbasus ut quondam magnis intenta theatris
> Dat crepitum, malos inter jactata, trabesque."
>
> *Lucretius*, VI. 107-109.

In both which passages the poet alludes not only to the upright "mali" or masts, but also to beams or rafters, as if, in addition to tension, some wooden frame-work or skeleton roof were made use of to sustain the cloth of the canopy. In colouring, sound, motion, and general effect, under a bright sun, and during a breeze of wind, we have nothing like what these enormous canopies must have presented, excepting, perhaps, a vast and gaily coloured balloon, when half filled with gas, upon a bright gusty day, rolling and wallowing from side to side, like an expiring sea-monster, with varying hues, and almost breathing noises. The undulating motion of the curtains of our largest theatres affords nothing beyond an agreeable whet to tiptoe expectation.

Note to page 125.

Juvenal's " nequeo monstrare et sentio tantùm,' is at first sight the only account to be given of the pleasure enjoyed in contemplating works of art, and especially sculpture; but a little consideration shews it to be analogous to the pleasure derived from a simile, which Dr. Johnson defines to be " the discovery of likeness between two actions in their general nature dissimilar, or of causes terminating by different operations in some resemblance of effect." And again, " A simile may be compared to lines converging in a point, and is more excellent as the lines approach from greater distance."—*Life of Addison*. And by a like operation of the mind, a block of marble, every way most unlike the living subject, becomes, under the hands of the sculptor, a most delightful object of contemplation, from the pleasing influence of *form alone;* for in sculpture, the effects of light and shade, and of perspective, are impossible; and any attempt at a closer approach to similarity by colouring would defeat its own purpose, and tend, like an exhibition of wax-work, to overwhelm the spectator beneath an ineffectual load of detail and lifeless exemplification.

Sculpture is pre-eminently distinguished by its purely abstract quality—its ideality—and its holding the letter in complete subjection to the spirit of the subject; nay, if it falls but little short of this degree of excellence, it is at once repudiated. And it is from these abstract properties of the art that the mind's eye acquires the power of restoring, as it were, a mutilated statue; for, provided the relic be *first-rate*, however its material shape may have been injured, the spectator will without effort recall the form of the original conception, as though it were immortal and indiscerptible.

And with all its high and abstract qualities, sculpture is necessarily tied down to rigorous accuracy of shape and outline. For who could endure disproportion or deformity in a statue? who bear to enter upon a physical question of thews and sinews, when called upon to feel deeply, and to generalise upon moral attributes? Moreover, a statue is, geometrically speaking, of three dimensions; and is, on that very account, brought into such palpable, close, unprotected contact, such immediate comparison, with surrounding objects and the breathing world, that it requires to be ensured from meeting with positive contempt by the magic influence of its abstract qualities, with which, as with a kind of divinity, it must be hedged about, or perish. The roughest design ever modelled — the rudest sketch ever dashed off — will be more pleasing than the finished statue which does *not quite* succeed. It is scarcely too much to say, that a sculptor ventures for complete success or total failure.

In painting the case is wholly different. Here the artist produces the effect by a knowledge of colouring, light and shade, and perspective, each, indeed, requiring separate study, but each contributing its distinct resources, combining at last in favour of the painter. Here many acknowledged faults are venial; not that the art has in itself no abstract quality — far from it; but because the faults can be artificially concealed, and, therefore, do not interfere with the delight of the spectator. In matters of art, " ce n'est pas pécher que pécher en silence."

Sculpture, as before stated, is of three dimensions; but painting is only of two, and is exhibited on an uniform plane surface; and is thus, as it were, carried into another region safely removed from the juxtaposition and interference of external objects; and, therefore, the lowest degrees of the art, down to the positively bad, and even wretched, will never be without advocates and supporters; because a picture never can cease altogether to be imitation — never through the meretricious blandishments of false taste can risk the entire loss of its denomination and character — a loss which infallibly befalls the sculpture that sinks below a certain limit, or oversteps the modesty of the rules naturally assigned to it by human feelings and perceptions. The " Transfiguration" of Raphael, and the veriest sign-post daub, are both of them pictures; but the Theseus of the Parthenon, and Wyatt's Newfoundland dog in variegated marbles, are not both statues.

Painting may, with all propriety, consist of large groups of figures; but, if an historical subject, for example, consisting perhaps of fifteen or twenty personages, were attempted to be represented in sculpture, though each particular figure might be admirably executed, yet the whole would be little better than a spectral assemblage, encroaching to an intolerable degree upon external objects. In one of the churches in the Netherlands the oaken sculpture about the pulpit is open to a similar objection. The subject is the calling of the fishers James and John by our Saviour. The figures stand too far from each other, and, what is worse, by an oaken sea-shore lies an *oaken boat*, to the entire destruction of the imitation, which at the same time would have been tolerably well preserved had the whole been constructed of marble. Yet such subjects as these might very properly be represented in basso-relievo, in which a multiplicity of figures is rescued from the interference of things around them, by their being, as in a picture, necessarily referred to one general plane surface. Hence it follows that the number of figures in a group of sculpture ought not to exceed two or three; and that the most intellectual efforts of the chisel are single figures. I am inclined to look upon the Laocoon less as a group, than as a single figure exquisitely *garnished.*

Again, for example, let Cupid chaining a lion be represented in sculpture. Agreeably to the abstract spirit, the relative proportions of the figures need not be sustained. The lion may with propriety be represented much smaller in proportion than the Cupid, for the object is to embody an allegory — the triumph of Love over brute force — and not the taming of a real lion by a child, which possibly such a group might assume the appearance of if exactly proportioned. But let the same subject be represented in a painting, and no such liberty can be taken with the relative proportions; for the art is endowed with accessories sufficient to secure it against misinterpretation, and is in return pledged to fidelity.

Sculpture, born to lofty flights, and unbounded range of thought, degenerates as soon as domesticated;

but painting by admitting a lower tone becomes fitted for the cabinet as well as the gallery. It has been observed of Chantrey, that his fancy subjects lost much of their intellectual intention after he had been long engaged in the execution of busts and portraits in marble: on the other hand, the poet Cowper's well-known effusion owes its tenderness to its being addressed to a painting. He would never have dwelt upon the scenes of his childhood, and introduced us into the very nursery, in lines penned to his Mother's *Statue*.

But when objects of three dimensions are injudiciously mingled with those of two, failure is sure to be the result. This may be seen in stage scenery, and in the branches of imitative art allied to it. Theatrical effects are essentially of three dimensions, and are produced by the joint agency of living performers and scenery; which latter is displayed bodily on a stage of both width and depth, but is unavoidably backed by a landscape or sky painted upon a plane surface, in fact, a picture; and is therefore somewhat of a mixed and ambiguous character; which, however, escapes remark so long as the interest of the audience is engrossed by the action and dialogue. But when the proper interest of the drama falls off, vain are the efforts made to elevate stage scenery into a source of real entertainment. Every one must have been struck by the incommensurable elements of imitation brought together in the moving panoramic views, with which, in spite of their cost and magnificence, the effect of our pantomimes is annually chilled; and I recollect once seeing some dwarfs or pigmies make their entry from what was intended to represent their diminutive dwelling, but which was painted on the front scene, and therefore looked like a dwelling of ordinary size seen in perspective at a considerable distance; so that a few steps carried the tiny actors to the very front of the stage over a seeming space of at least half a mile, to the confusion of all intelligible effect. Similar mistakes are committed by the introduction of such objects as water-wheels that revolve, streams that flow, and cottage chimneys that smoke, into the exhibition of the Diorama.

Tableaux vivants are the converse of paintings; they make solidity look like surface, and the real living subject stand for its own resemblance. From what has been said above, it is easy to see that they must be conducted with care and good taste, and that any injudicious introduction of accessories confounding them with stage effect would be fatal to the illusion. I remember a charming effect taking place quite accidentally in a *tableau*. One of two lovely young women who formed the group, fatigued no doubt by the attitude in which she was standing, unconsciously began to move, as if reanimated, like another Hermione, whilst her eyes lightened up, and a smile played about her lips, as she gazed upon her motionless companion, as if she were about to address her; and in that instant the curtain was let fall, leaving an impression on the mind more agreeable perhaps than any that fancy could have evoked from a bewitching and masterly painting.

In The Winter's Tale the spectacle of Hermione as a *painted Statue* is neither barbarous nor absurd in the representation, taken in conjunction with the dialogue, and arrangement of the scene. In the minds of the audience the injured Hermione yet lives; and on the stage even Leontes does not seem quite deceived by the artifice, but to be half addressing his words to *her ears*, and half to those of the surrounding personages. The manner too in which the harshness of the scene is softened down by his referring to Perdita, and so constituting her a connecting link between the *Statue* and the other characters present, together with Perdita's reply, is eminently beautiful.

> LEON. . . . . O, royal piece,
> There's magic in thy majesty, which has
> My evils conjured to remembrance, and
> From thy admiring daughter took the spirits,
> Standing like stone with thee!
>
> PER.   And give me leave;
> And do not say 'tis superstition, that
> I kneel, and then implore her blessing.
> *Winter's Tale, Act V. Sc. 3.*

In reading even these few lines we forget the inanimate *Statue*, and see only the wife and mother.

The conclusion intended to be drawn from these remarks is, that imitation addressed to the eye, whether effected by sculpture, painting, or stage effects, must, to be pleasing, possess a certain *unity of action;* and that the most abstract and perfect of these is sculpture.

But, since examples similar to those adduced will readily suggest themselves to every one, further endeavour to illustrate these points becomes superfluous.

Note to page 132.—*Trajan's Column.*

I cannot forbear quoting the latter portion of a short poem, by Wordsworth, addressed to this beautiful relic.

" Memorial Pillar! 'mid the wrecks of Time
   Preserve thy charge with confidence sublime—
The exultations, pomps, and cares of Rome,
Whence half the breathing world received its doom;
Things that recoil from language; that, if shewn
By apter pencil, from the light had flown.
A Pontiff, Trajan here the gods implores;
There greets an embassy from Indian shores;
Lo! he harangues his cohorts—there the storm
Of battle meets him in authentic form!
Unharnessed, naked, troops of Moorish horse
Sweep to the charge; more high, the Dacian force,
To hoof and finger mailed;—yet, high or low,
None bleed, and none lie prostrate but the foe;
In every Roman, through all turns of Fate,
Is Roman dignity inviolate;
Spirit in him pre-eminent, who guides,
Supports, adorns, and over all presides;
Distinguished only by inherent State
From honoured Instruments that round him wait;
Rise as he may, his grandeur scorns the test
Of outward symbol, nor will deign to rest
On aught by which another is depressed.
   Alas! that one thus disciplined could toil
To enslave whole nations on their native soil,

So emulous of Macedonian fame,
That, when his age was measured with his aim,
He drooped, 'mid else unclouded victories,
And turned his eagles back with deep-drawn sighs,—
O weakness of the great! O folly of the wise!
    Where now the haughty empire that was spread
With such fond hopes?—her very speech is dead;
Yet glorious Art the sweep of Time defies,
And Trajan still, through various enterprise,
Mounts, in this fine illusion, toward the skies:
Still are we present with th' imperial Chief;
Nor cease to gaze upon the bold Relief
Till Rome, to silent marble unconfined,
Becomes, with all her years, a vision of the mind."

We may couple with these lines the following passage from Gibbon.

"Trajan was ambitious of fame; and as long as mankind shall continue to bestow more liberal applause on their destroyers than on their benefactors, the thirst of military glory will ever be the vice of the most exalted characters. The praises of Alexander, transmitted by a succession of poets and historians, had kindled a dangerous emulation in the mind of Trajan. Like him the Roman emperor undertook an expedition against the nations of the East; but he lamented with a sigh that his advanced age scarcely left him any hopes of equalling the renown of the son of Philip."

I cannot, however, after an inspection of Bartoli's engravings of the Relief, quite admit that

"None bleed, and none lie prostrate but the foe."

And in one place some Roman soldiers that had been taken prisoners are represented as being tortured by the Dacian women, who are burning them in various parts of their bodies with lighted torches. To this day, among savage nations in various parts of the world, the women bear a part in tormenting and insulting their prisoners of war. In the first part of King Henry the Fourth are mentioned the outrages committed by the Welsh women at the defeat of Mortimer.

In the engravings the Dacians are represented with a national cast of countenance, which is kept up throughout; and I was strongly impressed with the idea that I recognised therein the cast of features I had previously observed among the Wallachians upon the Danube, about Orsova and Mehadia; but I cannot speak with certainty on a point with which accident and fancy may have much to do.

The Column of Marcus Aurelius is less celebrated; but among the sculptures thereupon is to be seen the very remarkable figure of Jupiter Pluvius, who is said to have interposed his miraculous assistance between the Roman army and that of the Quadi; in consequence, as believed by the Emperor himself at the time, of the prayers of his Christian soldiers. For, being in a most straitened condition, the Romans were saved from perishing from drought by a violent torrent of rain, whilst the Quadi were dispersed in terror with hailstones, and thunder and lightning.—*See* CREVIER's *Roman Emperors*, Vol. VII. Mill's Translation. *Lond.* 1814.

Note to page 136.—*The Lyons Mosaic.*

Unfortunately, my account of this remarkable mosaic is very imperfect. My companions complained of the cold of the place, and hurried me away; and I could not obtain any information from our attendant. An accurate drawing should accompany any written description of this mosaic. It is mentioned, and several of its details are specified, in Smith's Dictionary of Antiquities before referred to, *article* Circus.

I learn now that there were in this mosaic not six, but eight chariots represented; and in a rude sketch, which I began on the spot, but was prevented from finishing, I find depicted a double set of *Delphinæ*, four in each set, all spouting water. The *Ova* I seem to have omitted. In the passage, between the *Meta* and *Spina*, the extreme ends of the latter are not hollowed out into a circular recess, as they are in many examples. The slave, whom in the Journal I have perhaps too hastily described as standing ready to dash water over the chariot-wheels, is standing on the *alba linea* exactly in the situation of letter K in the woodcut in page 229 of Smith's Dictionary. Of this figure Artaud says, " Près les barrières est un homme à pied dans l'action de courir. Il est vêtu de vert, et tenant dans un bassin la somme destinée au vainqueur, qui est représentée par du lapis, comme une chose précieuse." And a little further on, he says of the horses, " Les chevaux se font remarquer par leur queue coupée à l'Anglaise." The two officials, with the garland and palm-branch, are standing in a wide passage in the centre of the *Spina*. The *Barrier* of the Tilt-yard seems to have derived its origin from the *Spina* of the Circus.

THE END.

LONDON:
PRINTED BY MOYES AND BARCLAY, CASTLE STREET,
LEICESTER SQUARE.

www.ingramcontent.com/pod-product-compliance
Lightning Source LLC
LaVergne TN
LVHW061214060426
835507LV00016B/1926